THE JOURNEY
OF
JOHN ENGLER

THE JOURNEY
OF
JOHN ENGLER

By Roger Martin, Nolan Finley and
The Detroit News Lansing Bureau
Charlie Cain, Mark Hornbeck and Yolanda Woodlee

Photographs by Audry Shehyn

A&M
Altwerger & Mandel Publishing Co., Inc.
6346 Orchard lake Road, Suite 201
West Bloomfield, MI 48322

Published by
A&M
Altwerger & Mandel Publishing Co., Inc.
6346 Orchard Lake Road, Suite 201
West Bloomfield, MI 48322

ISBN 1-878005-25-1 (cloth)
ISBN 1-878005-26-X (paper)

First Edition 1991

Designed by Mary Primeau

CONTENTS

PROLOGUE

It was 3:30 in the morning, and no one in Michigan was sure who would be governor when the sun came up.

Paul Hillegonds, sitting in his first-floor Capitol office, surrounded by stale coffee and fresh voter returns, reached for the telephone and dialed suite 1030 of the Lansing Radisson.

"How're you doing?" Hillegonds asked when John Mathias Engler answered.

"It's back and forth, but I'm gonna win. In fact, I'm going to bed, and I'm gonna sleep a couple of hours."

"John, how can anyone sleep under these circumstances?" asked Hillegonds, shocked by the calm in his old friend's voice.

"It's been that kind of campaign, and I'm totally at peace with the outcome," Engler answered. "I believe I'll be governor when I wake up. I know I'm going to win, and I want to look good on the Today Show."

As he hung up the phone, Engler settled back on his bed in

the three-room suite, smiled and repeated to himself, "I'm going to win this thing."

The 42-year-old Republican state senator from Mt. Pleasant had been saying that all along to anyone who would listen, to anyone who pumped his hand and took his pitch in each of Michigan's 83 counties. Few believed.

At that same moment, 90 miles away in downtown Detroit, 40-degree temperatures and shifting political winds were sending shivers through James Johnston Blanchard.

Blanchard's 16-year political undefeated streak, as well as his job, were in jeopardy. The power, the spotlight, the perks of office, could belong to someone else in a few hours. And not just anyone. The man sitting in his chair would be John Engler, his nemesis. For six years, Engler, as Senate majority leader, had criticized and blocked Blanchard's programs, and then launched a campaign to take his job.

Just a year earlier, in a private meeting with Hillegonds, the House Republican leader, Blanchard had boasted that Engler would never be governor: "The only thing he'll ever be remembered for is restoring the Capitol building."

Blanchard had looked forward to being rid of Engler after Election Day.

As Blanchard joined aides and would-be revelers at the International Center in Greektown, the swaggering confidence he'd shown during eight years as a congressman from Oakland County and eight more as Michigan's cheerleading governor was missing.

Already suffering from the flu, he had awakened Election Day to a case of bad news: His pollsters warned he was now trailing Engler, the first time in the race he had been behind. Once Michigan voters donned their coats and headed out to their precincts, exit polling showed the race a dead heat, startling news for Blanchard, whose lead was once more than 20 percentage points.

The doubts that dogged Blanchard and his top aides in

recent days now tormented the governor. Had the nasty campaign ads backfired? Had they ignored Detroit? Was there enough hand-to-hand campaigning? Was the anti-incumbency movement sweeping Michigan, too?

If everything had gone as planned, he would be celebrating now. Instead, as he watched the lead change hands with every new batch of returns, he was second-guessing. Maybe he could have better handled his announcement that the popular Lt. Gov. Martha Griffiths would not be his running mate? Perhaps he should have been more forceful on the abortion issue? Did his campaign ads do enough to trumpet his record?

Engler had no such doubts. His campaign had peaked at the right time, following a miserable September when it seemed Blanchard could do no wrong. Since mid-October, voters had been responding to the symbolic Engler nickel, the candidate's advertising campaign that emphasized the small cut that property owners would get from his opponent's tax relief plan.

Crowds had cheered Engler whenever he mentioned his trail-worn Oldsmobile, another symbol and one carefully crafted to contrast with Blanchard's helicopter travels. The state Republican Party had saved its money for a last-minute TV ad blitz. Anti-abortion forces had joined the state GOP in a massive and unprecedented get-out-the-vote phone effort.

The campaign had followed his carefully drafted plan to the letter.

On that morning, Engler had another reason to feel content. His proposal of marriage had been accepted in August by Michelle DeMunbrun, a Texas lawyer. No one outside their close circle of friends knew, but win or lose, they would marry Dec. 8.

Confidence alone doesn't win elections. It had been 28 years since Michigan voters turned out an incumbent governor, and Blanchard, though worried, had no reason to panic. While early returns from outstate Michigan showed Engler leading, it was generally assumed that the Democratic Detroit vote, usually counted late in the night, would carry Blanchard to victory.

It would, that is, if Detroit voted. Blanchard was shocked earlier by reports that only 12 percent of Detroiters had cast ballots by 4 p.m. Desperate, Blanchard hurriedly arranged to buy live, five-minute blocks of advertising time on Detroit's black-oriented radio stations to plead for votes just two hours before the polls closed. He repeated the plea during a lengthy, live interview with WXYZ TV-Channel 7 on the 5 p.m. newscast.

The race seesawed as votes were counted throughout the night and into Wednesday morning. At the Engler party in the Radisson, his backers gained confidence with each passing hour. Many didn't expect to be in the race past the evening hours.

By contrast, the Blanchard gathering was sullen until about 1:55 a.m. when a TV monitor showed the governor in front for the first time. Traditionally Democratic precincts in the large cities were finally coming in. A small knot of Blanchard loyalists, holding out until the end, let out a victory whoop.

But they howled in despair only moments later when new numbers showed Engler retaking the lead.

"Is John Engler really going to win this thing?" one young Blanchard supporter wearing a "Tough. Tested. Trusted" T-shirt asked no one in particular.

In a fourth-floor suite of private offices above a large conference room in the International Center at Greektown, Blanchard, his wife Janet, campaign manager Gary Bachula, and two long-time aides were staring at a bank of TV sets.

Nearby, a team of Blanchard loyalists, including legal adviser Mike Hodge and former lobbyist Larry Tokarski,

4

punched returns into computers. As the numbers came in, one aide recalled: "I felt a slug in my gut." Blanchard remained outwardly calm. He strained to be jocular. He kept checking the numbers.

Back at the Lansing Radisson, an adding machine spewed out a seven-foot-long paper tail of vote calculations to key members of the Engler team. The second-floor ballroom was strewn with beer bottles, empty pizza boxes, uneaten fruit, cold coffee and warm soda.

By 5:30 a.m., 20 people, those closest to Engler, were still hanging around. They had stuck it out through a roller coaster 18-month campaign. They were on the verge of triumph, just short of the biggest political upset in the nation, and they were not about to leave before the final curtain.

Near the table where election results were being taken by phone, state GOP Chairman Spencer Abraham studied a crude tally sheet covered with blue and red scribblings, which listed counted and uncounted precincts. State Sen. Connie Binsfeld, candidate for lieutenant governor, had said earlier that she wouldn't leave until she saw the stoic Abraham smile.

Like a holder of a winning Lottery ticket, Abraham checked his numbers against the winners and blinked once, then again. And then he smiled.

"I think we've won," Abraham whispered to his wife, Jane.

CHAPTER 1

John the Giant Killer

Revenge pushed John Engler into a career in politics.

In the spring of 1970, the 21-year-old Engler was just two months away from picking up a degree in agricultural economics from Michigan State University. But he had no intention of following in the boot prints of his father, a Beal City cattle farmer.

Nor did Engler intend to become a soldier. Like thousands of other draft-age males at colleges throughout the nation, Engler held tightly to an education deferment that kept him out of the jungles of Vietnam.

War protests swept the nation's campuses and streets, four students had just been mowed down by the bullets of National Guardsmen at Kent State in Ohio, and voters were bitterly divided over the U.S. military presence in Indochina.

Simon and Garfunkel's "Bridge Over Troubled Waters" spent six weeks atop Billboard's pop music charts. But while MSU was being rocked with anti-war sentiment, students also were rallying to get carpeting in Engler's East Shaw Hall dormitory and to ensure privacy following a relatively new campus rule allowing women in men's dorm rooms.

Engler had tasted political victory during his junior year at MSU in 1969, when he was elected Shaw Hall president. For his dorm constitutents, he had invented an "indoor curtain" to keep a couple's business private while technically adhering to the no-closed-doors rule.

His first flirtation with political campaigning had come in 1968, when his father, Matt, failed in his effort to oust seven-term state Rep. Russell Strange in the 100th House District Republican primary.

After the election, John Engler applied for jobs as a page and janitor at the state Capitol. When Strange found out about the job hunt, he blocked Engler's hiring. In the process, he made a dangerous enemy.

Strange, 35, was expected to coast to an easy win in 1970. As the filing deadline drew near, no one had come forward to challenge him in the August primary. He was the House Republican caucus chairman. He sat on the prestigious House Taxation Committee. A victory would place him third in seniority among his House GOP colleagues.

His confidence might have been shaken had Strange known how Engler was spending his spring. Seated at a desk in his dorm room, Engler carefully drafted a term paper for his political science class. The paper detailed how a challenger could knock off Strange.

No one, certainly not Engler, could know it then, but the 17-page report would serve as the blueprint for many future campaigns, including a run for Michigan governor two decades later.

The paper stressed the value of organization and long hours of hard work, just like on the farm.

"The challenger will only be able to win with a campaign of perspiration and participation," the student wrote.

He suggested that most issues would matter little in the race.

Of greater importance, the report concluded, was that Strange's remarkable 98-percent legislative attendance record in Lansing was keeping him away from the district, and he had lost touch with voters. Engler wrote that Strange considered his suburban Lansing residence as his home and only kept a "nominal" residence back in the district, "a house trailer placed on a lot." Ironically, by the end of his 20-year legislative career, Engler owned even less than that in the district.

Engler pointed out in the paper that the best way for the challenger to win was to become more familiar to district voters than Strange, and to play on his hometown roots. The challenger should cover the entire two-county district shaking as many hands as possible, Engler suggested.

"An issue-oriented campaign is neither sufficient nor totally desireable in an effort to unseat Rep. Strange," he wrote. "A massive campaign of personal contact may be anachronism in these days of mass media campaigning, but it is the best tactic available. The personal contact suggested is the people-to-people type."

As Engler pumped hands at district churches and farms, one issue he visited frequently was taxes. He bemoaned the "181-percent" increase in taxes during the previous decade, and he promised voters he would work to kill any tax hikes during his two-year term. A 30-second Engler radio spot drove the point home:

"John Engler says it's time to stop the state tax spiral. John Engler says it's time to reevaluate every dime of state spending."

In a bigger campaign two decades later, the pocket change symbol, this time a nickel, again paid dividends for Engler.

"There's a big parallel between that first campaign and the governor's race," said Sen. Dick Posthumus, who managed Engler's campaign against Strange as a 20-year-old college junior. "He started from day one working 18 hours a day and never stopped until it was done. And he always believed he would win."

9

Posthumus said that in the 1970 campaign, Engler campaigned until midnight, then sat up until 2 a.m. going over strategy for the next day. He'd be up at 6 a.m. to start all over again.

The term paper displayed an uncommon insight into politics and campaigns and a keen understanding of the many obstacles to beating an incumbent. The report earned Engler an "A" grade and a new job. Religiously following the plan he had laid out, Engler beat Strange 3,498 to 3,339. With a slim, 159-vote victory, just six months out of the classroom, the 22-year-old Engler was sworn in as the youngest of the 110-member Michigan House of Representatives.

He had avenged his father's loss and his own snubbing by Strange.

In 1972, Engler took on another entrenched incumbent.

Based on the 1970 U.S. Census, Michigan's political districts had been redrawn to reflect population changes. Engler's 100th District and state Rep. Richard Allen's 88th District in the heart of mid-Michigan now overlapped. Neither would voluntarily step aside.

Engler revised his plan slightly and with a 629-vote win sent Allen back to his farm and veterinary clinic. Fellow politicians began taking note of the chubby-cheeked Engler, who at age 24 had already deposed two incumbent lawmakers.

He wasn't finished.

He easily won re-election in 1974 and 1976 and began to gain both seniority and a reputation as a formidable campaign strategist. His reward was being named director of the state House Republican election committee, a position that gave him new power and influence. It also enabled him to assemble the staff that helped organize and manage the campaigns of other GOP candidates.

One of his early triumphs was helping unknown Colleen House of Bay City win a special state House election in June

1974. She became his wife in 1975, and they became a curiousity as the only husband-wife team in the Legislature.

Among those helping Engler on the House campaign was Colleen Meeuwenberg, a state House intern from MSU, and Dan Pero, a rising star on the GOP legislative staff. It was the beginning of a longtime political association between the three.

In 1978, Rep. Engler approached state Sen. Jack Toepp, a powerful 14-year veteran, and told him he wanted his job.

Toepp, a popular father of seven from Cadillac who did radio broadcasts of high school football games in his district, was taken aback by the bravado and tried to talk the ambitious Engler out of challenging him.

"Leave me alone this time," Toepp said, "and in 1982 I'll retire and endorse you as the man to replace me."

"No deal," said Engler, "Eight years in the House is long enough for me."

Again, Engler faced long odds and doubters. Toepp was the Republican Senate floor leader and a member of the powerful Appropriations Committee, which controls the state's purse strings. Toepp had recorded comfortable wins in his last two elections.

Engler won by 1,756 votes. A third incumbent had been slain, and the nickname, "John the Giant Killer" caught on.

The Republicans turned to Engler when longtime Gov. William G. Milliken decided to retire in 1982. The GOP wasn't looking to Engler as a candidate, but to help run the campaign of Richard Headlee, the Farmington Hills insurance executive and tax-cut advocate who in the primary had knocked off James Brickley, Milliken's lieutenant governor and hand-picked successor.

Headlee faced barely known U.S. Rep. James J. Blanchard from Oakland County, who had crushed his opposition to win the Democratic nomination.

A key GOP triumvirate was formed under the Headlee banner. Engler was co-chair of the campaign. Dan Pero, by now working for V. Lance Tarrance & Associates, Inc. of Houston, handled Headlee's advertising. Spencer Abraham was his pollster.

It was their first gubernatorial campaign.

And they blew it.

The conservative Headlee, charming, outgoing and an effective public speaker, had a tendency to shoot himself in the foot. Just days before the election, he remarked that sponsors of the Equal Rights Amendment were "proponents of lesbian marriage, homosexual marriage." His handlers could come up with no effective way of countering the resentment that remark created with women voters.

On Election Day, Blanchard collected 53 percent of the vote to become the 45th governor of Michigan.

Engler went back to the Senate, where he was rewarded with the post of minority leader. Although they had lost the governor's race, Republicans led by Engler added four seats to their Senate caucus. They were still the minority, but had narrowed the gap to just 20–18.

The events of the 14 months that followed dramatically changed Michigan politics and played a significant role in the outcome of the 1990 race for governor.

On Jan. 1, 1983, a formation of military jets screamed low heading east to west over the 105-year-old state Capitol. On the steps and lawn below, the crowd shivered in frigid temperatures as James J. Blanchard took the oath of office and headed with wife Paula for a gala reception in his honor.

The honeymoon was short. When Blanchard got the keys to state offices, he also got a checkbook that was $1.7 billion out of balance.

Blaming the deficit on the "voo-doo economics" of the Milliken administration, Blanchard recommended a 38-percent increase in the state income tax. It proved to be a rare display of leadership during the Blanchard years. It also proved to be one of the best things that ever happened to Engler's political career.

Blanchard's tax hike won legislative approval with only one Republican vote, that of Sen. Harry DeMaso of Battle Creek. Republicans, led by Engler, smelled Democratic blood. Across the state, the rumble from anti-tax groups grew louder and louder. Thousands of angry taxpayers began collecting signatures on recall petitions to oust Blanchard and Democratic lawmakers who voted for the tax hike.

In Lansing, the Republican power structure, while swearing publicly it was not involved in the messy recalls, plotted strategy, raised money for ads and did all it could to make certain angry voters stayed angry.

The recall efforts eventually zeroed in on two first-term Democratic senators who represented anti-tax hotbeds and who had won office by razor-thin margins. Oakland County voters went to the polls on Nov. 22, 1983, and recalled Sen. Philip Mastin. Eight days later, Macomb County voters dumped Sen. David Serotkin.

That night, Engler and a group of Republican revelers celebrated with champagne in the offices of Marketing Resource Group, a consulting firm in Lansing that had worked without charge on behalf of the recall groups.

On Jan. 31, 1984, Rudy Nichols of Waterford and Kirby Holmes of Utica swept into the Senate, making Republicans the majority party.

That made John Engler a very important man. Instead of being a minority leader with little real clout, he was now majority leader of the state Senate, able to control legislation and, to a large extent, determine how successful a governor Jim Blanchard would be.

The next day, Engler was so busy setting up the new Senate power structure he didn't have time to take a congratulatory call from Vice President George Bush.

CHAPTER 2

Young Boys Inc.

Jamie Blanchard's working-class neighborhood in suburban Pleasant Ridge was going big for Republican Dwight D. Eisenhower in 1952. But the 10-year-old Blanchard was an Adlai Stevenson man.

He took time out from his other boyhood passion, baseball, to peddle his bike to Stevenson's local headquarters to pass out literature for his idol.

Blanchard was raised by his mother, his father having abandoned the family when he was a young boy. His mother, Rosalie, was a Democrat and an admirer of liberal Michigan Gov. G. Mennen "Soapy" Williams.

Blanchard maintained his intense interest in politics at Michigan State University, where he was elected president of his sophomore and senior classes.

Like Engler, Blanchard learned to recognize populist political issues while a student at MSU. Blanchard pushed successfully to bring live rock music to campus, cigarette machines into residence halls and coeducational dorms. He

15

completed undergraduate work in social science in 1964 and earned an M.B.A. in 1965.

After earning a law degree at the University of Minnesota, Blanchard went to work for Democrat Attorney General Frank J. Kelley in 1969 and stayed five years until he beat an incumbent Republican congressman in 1974. Blanchard remained in Congress for eight years, during which time his crowning achievement was getting a federal loan to help Chrysler Corp. stay in business.

Blanchard rode his Chrysler fame to the governor's office in 1982, with solid support from union groups, blacks, women, and some backing from Detroit's suburbs. He quickly attracted the nickname "The Boy Gov," for his young age, 40, and youthful appearance.

His first four-year term was marked by the fallout from the unpopular 38-percent income tax increase. During a three-month drive in the spring and summer of 1983, just as Michigan was pulling out of a recession, anti-tax groups collected more than 400,000 signatures on petitions to recall him. They fell short, but many thought Blanchard would be a one-term governor.

Enter marketing and public relations pro Richard Cole. He was brought on board from the Lansing public relations firm he co-founded to help rescue Blanchard's sinking popularity. As press secretary and later chief of staff, the kinetic Cole was confident, amiable, smart and a backslapper. Cole became the personification of the feel-good, rah-rah tone of the Blanchard administration.

The administration shifted it's emphasis to image and promotion: Accentuate the positive, ignore the negative, and paint Michigan as "The Comeback State."

The strategy worked.

By Election Day 1986, Blanchard's fortunes, and the state's economy, had improved. The income tax rate had dropped back to 4.6 percent; people were returning to work;

16

and the Republican Party had chosen a weak candidate, Wayne County Executive William Lucas to run against Blanchard.

Blanchard walloped him.

By the start of his second term, Blanchard had surrounded himself with young, white, suburban Democrats.

Photos of their fallen heroes, President John F. Kennedy and former U.S. Attorney General and New York Sen. Bobby Kennedy, adorned the walls of offices from which Blanchard, state Treasurer Bob Bowman and campaign director Gary Bachula ran the state.

The Blanchard A-team, a small ring of advisers that included those people and a half-dozen or so others over the years, made their mark with big ideas and innovative programs.

But along the way, they became insulated, espousing their own middle-class brand of populism and forgetting the traditional, urban Democratic roots. Policy decisions emanated exclusively from the tight inner circle. They became sardonically known as Young Boys Incorporated to those on the outside.

Bachula described Blanchard as the "telephone governor," a leader who based policy decisions on advice from a variety of experts he would call any hour of the day.

"The idea that somehow two, three or four people insulated Jim Blanchard is not very accurate," Bachula said.

In Lansing, it was widely agreed that the lopsided victory over Lucas handed Blanchard a mandate that would allow him to push through his programs.

Instead, he squandered it. The win seemed to make Blanchard and his key aides overly confident, almost arrogant.

Most of the starters on the A-team had been together since

17

Blanchard's early days in Congress. Some go back even further:

- Bowman, a boyish Ivy Leaguer who helped then-Congressman Blanchard craft the bailout of cash-starved Chrysler Corp while he was at the U.S. Treasury. Bowman was the nation's youngest state treasurer when Blanchard hired him at age 28. He brought to the office a creative mind, an insatiable ego, a hair-trigger temper and a competitive nature.

- Shelby Solomon, Blanchard's budget director, a Blanchard congressional aide. Solomon, described as having Ken Doll good looks, offended many lawmakers during budget debates.

- Gary Bachula, a cerebral former aide to U.S. Rep. Bob Traxler of Bay City, who briefly shared his Capitol Hill desk with Congressman-elect Blanchard in 1974. The governor called upon Bachula, his friend, to manage the 1986 and 1990 re-election campaigns.

During their days in Washington, they gathered at the Dubliner Pub to share drinks and political banter.

When they held the reins of Michigan government, they pushed such programs as the prepaid college tuition plan and a savings plan to help first-time home buyers. Those measures and others largely benefited middle-class suburbanites like themselves. Blanchard and his aides understood the suburbs are home to millions of voters.

The governor also wooed some segments of the business community, which had become disenchanted with Republicans under the Milliken regime. The Business for Blanchard group included hundreds of business and industry leaders who kicked in thousands of dollars to his campaign and officeholder accounts.

In the spring of 1990, for the first time, Blanchard hosted a reception in his Mackinac Island mansion for the Greater

Detroit Chamber of Commerce, an unusual group for a Democratic governor in Michigan to entertain.

Traditional Demcocrats were aggravated by Blanchard's efforts to reach middle class and business interests. They felt it was coming at the expense of blacks, women, labor unions and advocates of the poor.

"I don't think labor knew what it was buying," said Rep. David Hollister, D-Lansing, referring to union's support of Blanchard in 1982. "I think he's more comfortable with the Lee Iacoccas than he is with the Joe Sixpack people from the unions or the party regulars."

By 1990, the inner circle was even tighter, and the insular attitude was reflected in the campaign. The governor did little personal campaigning. Despite protests from many of his closest advisers, he never appeared in person on TV ads. If the campaign could not control a public appearance, Blanchard simply ducked it. When he went door-to-door through suburban Detroit neighborhoods, a squad of aides stayed well ahead, knocking on the doors first to make sure their man would receive a favorable response.

"He should have done more grassroots, get-out-the-vote efforts. Not enough was put into this," said AFL-CIO Michigan President Frank Garrison.

His campaign became so exclusive that even some members of the A-team eventually lost the ear of the governor.

One aide said the governor's gatekeepers kept the gates closed and barred through much of the campaign. These guardians included Bill Liebold, his cabinet secretary and constant traveling companion; Jill Pennington, his director of operations; Tom Scott, the director of communications; and Steve Weiss, the tight-lipped and wary chief of staff.

When Blanchard did venture out, he favored travel by state helicopter. The helicopter became a ready symbol of the out-of-touch governor and his penchant for the trappings of office. Engler beat him over the head with it.

19

Blanchard's air travels accounted for about 75 percent of the state police jetcopter flights for the past two years. Between January 1989 and August 1900, Blanchard used the helicopter on 194 days. The aircraft costs a minimum of $750 an hour to operate. Most of his destinations were within a 90-minute drive of Lansing.

Many Blanchard supporters had assumed the governor would conduct his campaign like his highly successful, $243,000 tax-funded Great Lakes shoreline tour in the summer of 1989. He toured the 3,200-mile coastline by boat and car, stopping in dozens of cities, shaking hands, presenting plaques and posing for pictures with local residents.

"We all saw that as a warm up, the practice run," said Bill Castanier, a Labor Department spokesman and Blanchard appointee. "Wherever he went, thousands of people showed up to shake his hand and talk to him. He was signing autographs, for Christ sake."

But then Blanchard suddenly disappeared from the campaign trail, and even people in the administration began calling him the imperial governor.

"From July to August, what was Blanchard doing?," said one aide. "He just shut down. He was invisible, and none of us could figure out exactly why."

CHAPTER 3

Plan the Work.
Work the Plan

John Kost fits the image of the All-American boy: tall, blond, blue-eyed, Nordic handsome. He greets visitors with a firm handshake and a warm smile.

You'd never know he is a political assassin.

Kost works for John Engler, and his job during the gubernatorial campaign was to keep track of everything Jim Blanchard did or said, and then find ways the governor's own record and words could be used to defeat him.

He started the task in January 1987, just days after Blanchard took the oath for his second term. The next election was nearly four years away. Yet Kost and a half dozen or so other Engler allies already were planning Engler's 1990 campaign.

Eventually, Kost's job description, officially called opposition research, was spelled out in a 192-page campaign blueprint that detailed everything that had to be done if Engler was to defeat a popular, incumbent governor.

Kost, a long-time Engler detail man, headed Engler's clandestine research team, which had developed a special computer program designed to execute two key missions.

"We examined Blanchard's record, where he was strong and weak, from Congress on," Kost said. "And we put together Engler's record, so that we knew how he would be attacked."

Kost and staff uncovered and entered into the computer nearly every single vote Blanchard cast while in Congress. They tracked whether his policy decisions had worked or failed. They recorded all Blanchard quotes published in newspaper articles.

In essence, they gathered mud to throw during the campaign.

They twisted statistics to cast their foe in the worst possible light. They tried to be better at their job than the Blanchard aides who were doing the same thing across the street in the state Capitol.

In sifting through Blanchard's promises and programs, Kost stumbled across a nugget. Using the Unisonic XL-133 calculator on his desk, Kost figured out that Blanchard's property tax relief plan would yield a weekly savings of just 5.02 cents.

A nickel.

Kost passed on the find to Engler's media managers, who built an ad campaign around it.

The veracity of Kost's findings were questioned by some, but the impact of the nickel message could not be denied.

"The nickel was a very effective image," said Julie Dade, Blanchard's Detroit office director. Folks who were supporters of Blanchard would say to me, 'What's the governor doing about this?' "

As Kost was digging for dirt in late 1987, a tight band of Engler confidantes also was doing early campaign planning in a ninth-floor office in the Capitol Hall Building in downtown Lansing.

They called themselves the Saturday Morning Group, named after the first day they met in the fall of 1987.

Those who gathered in the offices of Marketing Resource Group, a GOP consulting firm, included Tom Shields, the affable president of the firm; Jerry Crandall, Engler's chief of staff; LeAnne Redick, the Engler staffer who specialized in organizing people; and Gail Torreano, Engler's executive assistant, close friend and former chief of staff. David Doyle, director of caucus services for Senate Republicans and a marvel at political strategy, also attended occasionally, as did state GOP Chairman Spencer Abraham.

And of course, Engler was there. By now, it had become clear that he was deeply interested in running for governor, although he had made no final decision. It was equally clear that he had problems. The Saturday Morning Group was charged with taking an ambitious but flawed candidate and weaving him into gubernatorial material.

"We sort of set a course that showed John some of the things that needed to be done if he were to run for statewide office," Shields said. "We basically sort of served as the political advisers he's never had before."

The Saturday Morning Group was blunt in its assessment of the potential candidate.

In Lansing, Engler had earned a reputaton as an insider, an obstructionist to everything that Blanchard wanted to do, a back-room dealer who stopped at nothing to get his way and bury his foes. He was a poor public speaker. Every smile appeared forced. He was too serious. Worse still, he was virtually unknown outside mid-Michigan.

In 1988 and 1989, the group reviewed lists of events going on around the state and sent Engler to those that helped improve his stature and name identification. They closely analyzed the condition of local GOP committees in each county and shored up those that were weak. They reviewed lists of special interests, including farm, ethnic, religious and anti-tax groups, to plot ways Engler could win their favor.

"OK. What are we doing with all these grass roots groups? How can we help them?" Engler asked at one of the meetings.

Every so often, Engler raffled off a gift to a group member whose name was drawn from a hat. Gifts included pens, sweatshirts, bags of apples, whatever gratuity Engler collected at speaking engagements. Engler is a noted gift giver. Mackinac Island fudge is routinely delivered to staffers. Female workers often come into the office to find fresh flowers on their desks.

"This is the side of you that you have to show out there," one member of the Saturday Morning Group told Engler.

The group concluded that Engler needed to soften his image. The state Republican Party had to unite behind Engler, because there was no room for a challenger who could divide party loyalties. Also, Engler needed to raise campaign money early so he could devote 1990 to the arduous task of campaigning.

"He was doing the sorts of things that would preclude serious consideration of campaigns for governor by other candidates," said Abraham.

At least four other prominent republicans were eyeing a run: State Sen. Edgar Fredricks of Holland, Rep. Bill Bryant of Grosse Pointe Farms, Grand Rapids businessman Dick DeVos and Detroit lawyer Clark Durant. But each backed out after seeing how far ahead Engler was in terms of organization and fundraising.

The Saturday Morning Group kicked off fundraising with a birthday bash for Engler's 40th on Oct. 12, 1988. It brought in more than $88,000 and was an encouraging gauge of his political appeal and his ability to raise money.

Guest invitations were printed on record jackets with the song "Johnny Engler," a goofy takeoff on the 1950s hit "Johnny Angel":

24

"Johnny Engler's turning 40

"And he's starting to show signs of wear.

"He's putting on some weight and losing some of his hair."

More silly songs and birthday parties were in Engler's political future. In 1989, birthday tickets cost $100 and raised $214,830.

Standing unnoticed in the Kellogg Center at the 1989 party, among the Engler staffers, lobbyists and executives of companies who do business with the state, was a tall man with slightly graying hair. Political consultant Dan Pero, who had flown back to his home state from Houston to eye job opportunities, was impressed with what he saw.

Thirteen years earlier, Pero had stood at the altar of the River Terrace Christian Reformed Church in East Lansing and watched his bride approach. "I do," was not the only thing Colleen Meeuwenberg heard from her beau on that November afternoon in 1976.

As the couple turned to take their vows, Pero stooped and whispered to Meeuwenberg, "Doug Bailey called me today. Can you believe it!"

Bailey was the top partner in the Washington Republican consulting firm of Bailey, Deardourff & Associates. Three days after the wedding, Pero hopped in his 1974 red-and-black AMC Gremlin and drove through the night to make his 9 a.m. job interview with Bailey.

He got the job and moved into a furnished Washington apartment with no carpeting, a bed so soft it sunk to the floor and heating pipes beneath the floor that burned unsuspecting feet. She stayed behind to finish her undergraduate degree at MSU before heading to the nation's capital to work for Youth for Understanding, the largest high school student exchange program in the country.

Over the next 14 years, their careers brought them back to

25

Michigan, to Washington again, to Arizona and eventually to Houston. Colleen completed graduate school in Phoenix, went to work for Gulf Oil and then got her law degree. Dan joined a Texas consulting firm and later opened his own communications business. Their jobs, which kept them in different states most of the time, led them to divorce court in June 1984.

The Peros remarried in September 1987 and moved back to Michigan in January 1989 to become linchpins in the Engler-for-Governor machine. Their return fulfilled a promise they had made to Engler a decade earlier.

The lesson Pero brought with him from Bailey, Deardourff was simple: Plan the work, and work the plan.

From February to May 1989, he would stretch out on the floor of his Okemos house, and, on yellow and white legal pads, scribble the Engler for Governor blueprint. It was 192 pages typed. It built on all the early work done by Kost, the Saturday Morning Group and others. Throughout the drafting, Engler peeked over his shoulder, suggesting changes and revisions.

Seven copies of the plan were distributed in late spring 1989 to the GOP brain trust for comment. The near-final draft was completed a few weeks later. The basic tenets of the plan were:

- Raise money early; hold enough back to make a final October push.
- Paint Blanchard as an imperial governor who wallows in the perks of office.
- Make personal appearances in every county in the state.
- Pace the campaign so that it peaks on Election Day.

One of Pero's tasks was to assess the strengths and weaknesses of the candidate and to pick the people to run the campaign. Like the Saturday Morning Group, Pero realized that Engler was perceived as an "aloof, back room deal-

John Engler and Ronna Romney talk on the phone early in the morning after Engler claimed his victory. Behind him is his press secretary, John Truscott, and campaign driver, Dave Bertram. Audrey Shehyn Photo

Buck Rogers of St. Clair Shores was one of the holdouts at Blanchard's Greektown headquarters election night. The changing lead caused it to be an all night affair. Diane Weiss Photo

John Engler surveys the packed room of supporters and reporters in Lansing as he enters his first press conference as governor-elect. Audrey Shehyn Photo

One of Engler's early triumphs was helping unknown Colleen House of Bay City win a special state House election in June 1974. She became his wife in 1975, and they became a curiousity as the only husband-wife team in the Legislature. In 1986 State Representative Colleen Engler announced her candidacy for governor of Michigan. Ed Lombardo Photo

Blanchard attracted the nickname "The Boy Gov," for his young age, 40, and youthful appearance when he took office in 1982. His first four-year term was marked by the fallout from the unpopular 38-percent income tax increase. During a three-month drive in the spring and summer of 1983, just as Michigan was pulling out of a recession, anti-tax groups collected more than 400,000 signatures on petitions to recall him. They fell short, but many thought Blanchard would be a one-term governor. Detroit News Photo

John Engler, center foreground, is surrounded by his campaign "brain trust", from left, John Truscott, Tom Shields, LeAnne Redick, Richard McLellan, (back row from left) Colleen Pero, Dan Pero, Dennis Schornack and Jeff McColvey. Audrey Shehyn Photo

The Nickel became an important campaign issue and symbol. Audrey Shehyn Photo

John Kost, Senate
Republican policy staff
director, was the man
who figured out that
Blanchard's property
tax relief plan would
yield a weekly savings
of just 5.02 cents — or a
nickel. Audrey Shehyn
Photo

The Plan, a 192-page
blue-print that detailed
everything that had to
be done if Engler was
to be successful,
required that John
Truscott, Engler's press
secretary, promptly
return all press calls
because favorable cov-
erage would be critical.
Audrey Shehyn Photo

Engler had earned a reputation as an insider, an obstructionist . . . a backroom dealer who stopped at nothing to get his way and bury his foes. UPI Photo / David Olds

HAPPY 40th

JOHN ENGLER

"And he's starting to show some signs of wear / He's putting on some weight and losing some of his hair." Lyrics to "Johnny Engler" a take off on the song "Johnny Angel."

From left, LeAnne Redick, Colleen and Dan Pero. The Peros have been long time associates of Engler. Audrey Shehyn Photo

Donald Bailey stands in front of his home where a throng of local leaders and residents trooped on the night of Feb. 9, in downtown Tekonsha. These were the new Republican activists whom The Plan said could make Engler governor. Audrey Shehyn Photo

Martha Griffiths addressed the Michigan Women Voters after Blanchard removed her from the ticket on Aug. 27. Joe Devera Photo

Connie Binsfeld provided
Engler stability on the
ticket—an alternative to the
Blanchard-Griffiths fallout.
Audrey Shehyn Photo

"I did not know (the commercial) was to be for John
Engler. I wanted publicity for
business, I was not doing it
for money." Naji Alaassri,
Lafayette Coney Island.
Audrey Shehyn Photo

The TV ad run by the Blanchard team depicting a white guard shouting at a black inmate at the state's military-style boot camp resulted in charges and counter-charges of racism. It was later referred by Blanchard aides as, "that (bleeping) ad."

Engler campaigns at Detroit's Eastern Market during what his aides called "the month from hell." Dale Young Photo

Engler stood next to an empty podium in Traverse City, during the first of three debates with Gov. James Blanchard. Blanchard refused to come out for the photography session prior to the debate. Kirthmon Dozier Photo

maker who cared more about the political process than good public policy."

Aides also were raising concerns about Engler's girth and appearance. His struggles to lose weight were well known. He had tried liquid diets, popcorn diets and planned menus to no avail. The exercise bike in his East Lansing condominium bedroom had become a clothes rack. Use it, he was told. On the campaign trail, Engler brought along apples and bananas to get him past the roadside hamburger joints. Before TV ads were filmed, Engler was convinced to trim his bushy black eyebrows, "Spock-like," one campaign adviser called them.

Money drove the plan. Both Engler and Blanchard accepted public campaign funds, limiting each man to $3 million to cover costs in the primary and general elections. Eight of every 10 dollars would be spent on television ads, Pero figured, so the rest of the campaign had to be lean. There was no money for yard signs, billboards, visors, buttons and other traditional trinkets paid for by the campaign. When requests were made for those and other items, Pero responded: "No. It's not in the plan."

The other key theme of the plan dovetailed with the skimpy campaign budget: Engler, the regular guy, versus Blanchard "the imperial governor."

While the incumbent governor flew from stop to stop in taxpayer-funded helicopters and planes, Engler put 60,000 miles on his 1988 Oldsmobile and another 60,000 miles on the campaign's red Chevy Astro Van, nicknamed Starship Enterprise.

This contrast was never more evident than on the Fourth of July parade circuit. Both candidates finished working the Clawson parade about the same time and headed to another parade in Wyandotte. Engler was in his van, Blanchard was in the jetcopter. Engler driver Dave Bertram described the race:

"We were getting into the van just as they were getting into the jetcopter. We could see them in a field near the parking lot. I said to John, 'Looks like this is a true race between the van and the jet copter. We drove down I-75, and, for a while, we had the copter spotted. I was going pretty fast, but we couldn't keep up. I don't how much we lost the race by because they were out of view after a while. We ended up near the end of the parade, they were near the beginning.' "

The hare had beaten the tortoise, this time.

To save money, the plan called for Engler to bypass overnight stops at the Holiday Inn and spend nights on the road in the homes of supporters, some everyday folks, such as Bob and Norma Pack of Oscoda and Gwen and Jackie Cowles of South Haven.

For four days while campaigning in Michigan's thumb, Engler commandeered the room of 5-year-old Stephen DeGrow, son of state Sen. Dan DeGrow, a Port Huron Republican. The room was papered with posters of the Detroit Pistons and Teenage Mutant Ninja Turtles. DeGrow's 8-year-old daughter asked Engler in early May to make her a promise: That he'd throw a tea party for her at the governor's residence on Mackinac Island. Engler gave her a card that said, "One tea party for Allison DeGrow" and told her: "Save this. It'll be worth something." It was signed "Gov. John Engler."

In an effort to shore up the base that had slipped away from Republicans in recent years, the plan told Engler to visit each of Michigan's 83 county courthouses. Shake hands and slap the backs of long-neglected local officials. He made his courthouse trek between July 14, 1989, and Jan. 22, 1990. Before the campaigning ended, he had visited some counties more than a half dozen times.

"We were in courthouses where I was told that candidates for statewide office hadn't been in 40 or 50 years," Engler said.

His first stop was in White Cloud (between Grand Rapids and Traverse City) at the Newaygo County Courthouse, a rickety building that went up in 1907 and hasn't changed much since. Over the next 12 months, Engler visited the county two more times. On May 4 he dined with Republicans at the annual Lincoln Day dinner, and on July 21 he joined in the region's celebration of its heritage at Old Fashioned Days.

The plan told Engler to show up at similar community events throughout the state and walk the main streets of small town Michigan. Newaygo County Sheriff Roger Altena was impressed.

"I can't ever remember Blanchard being in our county, and he was asked a number of times," Altena says. "Engler was there three times in a year."

On the night of Feb. 9, a throng of local leaders and residents trooped to Don and Lois Bailey's house at Main and North streets in downtown Tekonsha, a pea-sized hamlet south of Battle Creek. These were the new Republican activists the plan said could make Engler governor.

Lois served hot apple cider, finger sandwiches and vegetables and dip. After mingling with the crowd, Engler called them to attention and said: "Get the vote out. If we get the vote out in the rural areas, we can do it."

Don Bailey, the village president, later served as co-chair of Engler's Calhoun County election team. He helped convince rural Republicans to support Engler, and he set up a phone bank in his circa-1898 Victorian-styled house to get voters to the polls on Election Day.

"We talked about the need to engage in an early process of building his strengths among Republicans," said GOP Chairman Abraham. "You no longer need to get a lot of Democrats to win a statewide election. If you hold your base and win the majority of independents, you can win the election."

The plan told Engler to focus late in the campaign on the voter-rich suburbs, where property taxes were of paramount concern. Also, it instructed him to seek the active support of

29

anti-abortion groups and of farmers and ethnic groups, such as Metro Detroit's Polish and Arab American communities.

The blueprint even told him to work Detroit, enemy territory for Republicans. Over the years, Engler had forged a working relationship with Mayor Coleman A. Young. Engler campaigned in black churches, attended candidate nights at inner-city community centers and schools and he, not Blanchard, showed up at the Feb. 17 Barristers Ball, one of Detroit's top black social functions.

"Engler stole the show," said Jerome Barney, who invited Engler to the lawyers' event. Here's the governor, who's a Democrat and whose natural constituency is black, and he wasn't there. Engler was.

"Engler took pictures with Tommy Hearns, Aretha Franklin, who was Coleman Young's date. Engler shook hands with Young. He's a natural.

"He stayed for a couple of hours. He had on a black tuxedo. Engler had asked if he could come in a business suit, we told him to wear a tux so he wouldn't offend anyone. We arranged a special room in the Westin so he could change. He said he hates to wear a tux."

Young, who endorsed Blanchard, kept a dialogue going with Engler throughout the campaign.

"I met with him many, many times," Young said. "He indicated that he would be (responsive) to Detroit all during his leadership. He came down every 15th of January for the Martin Luther King birthday celebration. That was unusual for anybody from the state, any non-Detroit representative."

Along with Pero, the campaign team consisted of:
- Colleen Pero, 35, liaison between Engler's state Senate office and the campaign. She made sure all phone calls and letters from constituents were answered, and that

Engler was in the Senate, not on the campaign trail, during state business hours.

- Andrea Fischer, 32, fundraising chair. She knows the big shooters in the Republican Party and in Metro Detroit business and industry circles.

- LeAnne Redick, 28, political director. She organized at least one Engler team in each of the 83 counties. The teams handed out literature at front doors and at community events, raised money, made phone calls, and pinpointed parades, dinners, fairs and other events that Engler attended.

- Abraham, 38, and Doyle, 32, of the state GOP, key strategists. They developed Engler TV ads that were funded by the party, helped pick the rest of the ticket, and made sure get-out-the-vote teams were in place throughout the state.

- John Truscott, 24, press secretary. The plan told him to return all press calls promptly because favorable coverage would be critical.

In addition to running the campaign, Pero faced the unenviable task of trying to win the confidence and respect of some GOP doubters. Some party insiders said privately that the years Pero spent in Texas and Washington may have left him out of touch with Michigan politics. Others expressed concerns that Pero had closed the inner circle, shutting out party regulars.

More than anything, the plan told the Engler team to never stray far from its beacons, even in the face of adversity and criticism from allies, and even at times when the campaign appeared out of fuel.

"I've seen campaigns spend thousands of dollars for elaborate plans and then immediately walk away from them," Engler said during the campaign. "I think the much more certain route to success is to have a plan and stick to it. A simple plan that's 100 percent executed will always beat a comprehensive plan that's only 10 percent accomplished."

It was a bone-chilling 16 degrees on the banks of the Boardman River near the Grand Traverse County Government Center in downtown Traverse City on Feb. 12, Abraham Lincoln's birthday. John Engler's hands were numb, making it hard to turn the pages of his speech. The words came easily, though.

Michigan's unemployment rate is 8.4 percent, "highest in America," Engler told the crowd. "Drop out rates are up. Test scores are down. Welfare spending is up. The people deserve more than a nickel a week in property tax relief, which is all the governor has proposed. You could save for a month, and that wouldn't even buy you a pack of gum."

He took his announcement speech that day to Grand Rapids, Midland and Detroit, finishing near dusk on the steps of the state Capitol, directly below the second-floor offices of Gov. James J. Blanchard. On the sill of one open window, a Blanchard aide had placed a tape recorder to capture the rival's words.

Matt Engler, the candidate's father, thought to himself, "I wish I had dressed warmer."

To the rear of the crowd stood a solitary figure, the man who had quarterbacked Blanchard's 1986 re-election landslide over Bill Lucas. Gary Bachula, who had just signed on to run another Blanchard for Governor campaign, was taking mental notes.

As always, political strategy dominated his thoughts. Among the questions he was mulling: What to do about Martha?

CHAPTER 4

The Running Mates

Martha Griffiths, at age 78, clearly was past her prime.

Whispers about the lieutenant governor could be heard everywhere in the Capitol.

The former firebrand congresswoman needed one, sometimes two escorts to climb stairs. In her duties as president of the state Senate, she rarely lasted past noon. She had trouble hearing even at close range. Her mental sharpness was questioned.

Rumors persisted that she had had a stroke, or that she was suffering from Alzheimer's disease, or that she drank too much.

Her husband, Hicks, eventually admitted that she had been treated for a bleeding ulcer, but refused to release her medical records when Gov. Blanchard and reporters pressed for them.

It was clear that Blanchard wanted Griffiths off the 1990 ticket. But it had to be done gracefully. Blanchard would be the villain if a fight to dump the grand dame of the state Democratic Party became public.

She was the first woman to serve on Detroit Recorders Court. During her 20 years in Congress, she was among the most powerful women in the country, and she became Michigan's first elected woman lieutenant governor.

In Congress, she led the national effort to pass the Equal Rights Amendment and was a champion of civil rights. She had worked tirelessly to include the word "sex" in the 1964 Civil Rights Act to prevent gender-based job discrimination. In the late 1940s, when the state party was in shambles, she and Hicks and a small band of reform-minded liberals rebuilt it, and then put Soapy Williams in the governor's office.

Her apppeal to women, senior citizens, blacks and liberals had helped Blanchard beat Richard Headlee in 1982.

"I won that election for him," she said often.

Blanchard often dodged the question of whether Griffiths would be his 1990 running mate. "It's her decision," was his stock response. When she made her decision, it shocked Blanchard and nearly everyone else.

Griffiths scheduled a rare news conference on May 10 at the University Club in East Lansing. Newspapers across the state, quoting Democratic Party leaders, carried headlines claiming she intended to announce her retirement.

But at the news conference, Griffiths said: "I have experience; I am qualified; and I am available. If the governor and the Democrats believe I can be of help and strength to the ticket, I am ready, able and willing to serve a third term."

"Don't you think this puts the governor in a tough spot?" Griffiths was asked.

"That's tough," she bellowed.

Griffiths' strained relationship with Blanchard in the three months that followed her surprise announcement was much like the previous three years. They rarely spoke. He failed to return numerous phone calls from her.

On Aug. 27, Blanchard met Griffiths in her room at an Ann Arbor hotel and said he was removing her from the ticket. Griffiths was so angry she would not speak to the governor. Later that day, Blanchard called reporters to his Capitol office and announced that he had done what no one thought he had the courage to do.

"The lieutenant governor must be ready at a moment's notice to step in and take over the heavy responsibility of being governor should anything unforeseen happen to me," Blanchard said. "With this in mind I base my decision solely on what is best for the people of Michigan and the future leadership of this great state."

Although few argued the merits of the decision to oust Griffiths, most agreed that Blanchard had handled it poorly. CBS personality Connie Chung put a scorned Griffiths on national TV, and the New York Times ran a story sympathetic to her on its front page.

Still, Blanchard now was free to make his choice. But not as free as he would have liked. If Griffiths had followed Blanchard's game plan and stepped aside, he could have sized up a number of qualified running mates. He also could have been a king-maker. Blanchard said he had no intention of seeking a fourth term, so whomever he chose as lieutenant governor had the inside track to succeed him.

Blanchard was looking at Macomb County Prosecutor Carl Marlinga, someone who could deliver votes in a pivotal county, and Treasurer Bob Bowman.

"The governor thinks very highly of Bowman," said Blanchard campaign manager Gary Bachula. "He thinks of him almost like a protege. He imparted much of his political savvy to Bob, and there was a feeling that Bowman would provide continuity in the governor's office. The governor thought, 'Here's a person who thinks like I do, shares my ideas and values and could grow to be gubernatorial material.' In a total political vacuum, I think he would have liked Bowman to be on the ticket."

But Blanchard needed a woman on the ticket, particularly once Engler made his running mate choice.

Paul Hillegonds was feeling the pressure. For several weeks starting in early July, the state's GOP leadership had been working him over. As a popular lawmaker from Republican-rich western Michigan, Hillegonds could help bring the GOP base to the polls on Election Day. He had a reputation for political moderation, honesty, intelligence and energy.

Join the ticket, he was prodded by Engler and Party Chairman Spencer Abraham, and help John win.

But Hillegonds had concerns of his own. As Republican leader of the state House, he wanted someday to help his party take the majority so he could be speaker. He believed the gubernatorial running mate should be a prominent Republican from Metro Detroit, where Engler was little known. Someone like former Oakland County Prosecutor L. Brooks Patterson.

Hillegonds also read the polls like everyone else. The numbers gave Engler little chance, and a loss now would short-circuit a promising political future for the 41-year-old Holland lawmaker.

After 10 days of deliberation, Hillegonds brought bad news with him when he walked into Engler's Senate office at 11 p.m. one night in late July. In the room were Engler, Abraham and campaign boss Dan Pero.

Hillegonds wished Engler luck but said: "I just want to be removed from consideration."

So, how about Brooks Patterson?

His law-and-order reputation played well in Oakland and Macomb counties. On the stump, his quick wit and charm were unequaled in the state GOP. Of all the potential running mates being considered, Patterson was by far the most popular, internal party polls showed.

On the down side, his charismatic personality would overshadow Engler. Also, Patterson was best known for his rabid support of the death penalty, which Engler strongly opposed.

Patterson had recently formed a new law firm with some friends. During a late August meeting in Oakland County with Abraham and Engler, Patterson said he could not bail out on his partners, even to be Engler's running mate. Some speculated that Patterson was miffed that Engler's invitation had not come sooner.

But party insiders viewed those as convenient excuses masking the real reason, which was Patterson's desire to run for Oakland County executive in 1992 when Dan Murphy is expected to retire.

Patterson undoubtedly thought he could not afford to be saddled with another political loss. In 1982, he was beaten by Richard Headlee in the primary for governor. That same year he was nominated for attorney general and was buried by Frank J. Kelley.

Patterson told Engler to find someone else.

"The timing was too difficult for me," Patterson said.

Call central casting and ask for a grandmother, and they might send Connie Binsfeld. Few expected her to get an audition for the role of running mate.

The 66-year-old state senator from Maple City, northwest of Traverse City, often was seen knitting on the chamber floor during long sessions. Her nickname among the capital press corps was "Mrs. Butterworth," after the matronly looking woman on the pancake syrup bottle. In 1977, the mother of five and grandmother of three was chosen Michigan Mother of the Year.

That Engler would even consider Binsfeld raised eyebrows given their spat in 1986, when he ousted her from a key Senate leadership post and replaced her with his long-time pal and first campaign manager, Sen. Dick Posthumus of Alto.

The choice of Binsfeld also made little political sense because she and Engler would form a ticket of out-state senators with no strong connection to voters in southeastern Michigan.

But she is a woman and a senior citizen, and Blanchard was in the process of jilting a high-profile lieutenant governor with those same credentials. Binsfeld and Engler also shared many beliefs, including a steadfast opposition to abortion. And Binsfeld was a safe choice. She would be steady on the campaign trail, work hard and not eclipse Engler.

Connie and John Binsfeld were in their blue ranch house on Glen Lake one night in late August, watching the sun disappear behind the Sleeping Bear sand dunes. The phone rang. It was Engler.

They chatted in general terms about the advantages of having a woman on the ticket and decided that gray hair wouldn't hurt, either.

"Well, I've made my decision," Engler said. "I want you to be my running mate."

"John, I would love to do it," she answered.

About 150 miles to the northeast, Democratic state lawmakers were gathered on Mackinac Island with Blanchard. They roundly chuckled when told of Engler's choice of Binsfeld. They viewed her as a political lightweight who did nothing to shore up Engler's weakness in southeast Michigan.

They weren't laughing, however, about new and damaging comments aimed at Blanchard by a bitter Griffiths. In interviews with reporters published that day, she suggested that the governor was a "son of a bitch" for booting her off the ticket.

The Griffiths debacle and Engler's choice of Binsfeld left Blanchard with one choice: Olivia "Libby" Maynard, who had been on the ticket once before.

In 1978, Maynard became the first woman in Michigan history to be nominated as lieutenant governor. She ran on the failed ticket of William Fitzgerald, a Detroit Democrat who lost to Bill Milliken.

Maynard, 54, was director of the state Office of Services to the Aging, which tends to the interests of Michigan's 1.4 million senior citizens. Maynard would help soothe resentment among seniors who were partial to Griffiths.

Like Binsfeld, Maynard was a safe choice. She was loyal and would not embarrass the governor on the campaign trail. She had strong roots in the state Democratic Party, having served as its chair from 1979 to 1983. She was a darling of the powerful labor unions. She was from Flint, in Genesee County, where an important slice of the Democratic base lives and works.

"Once her name was mentioned she seemed like the best option," said Katie Wolf, campaign press secretary.

Blanchard said: "I trusted Libby. I still do. She was highly regarded in human service areas, where I was weak."

On Sept. 5, the clumsily managed coup was over. Blanchard announced that Maynard was in. Griffiths was out.

A month later, Griffiths was sitting in her chair in the Senate chamber, listening to yet another long-winded debate. She had heard enough and decided to duck out.

Dennis Schornack, Engler's policy chief, was leaving the chamber at the same time. He held open the door to the elevator behind the Senate chamber.

"Thank you," the lieutenant governor said to Schornack. "By the way, that nickel ad, I just love it."

CHAPTER 5

Ad Wars

Gov. Jim Blanchard dropped into Lafayette Coney Island three days before the election. He ordered a hot dog, a soft drink and an explanation from Naji Alaassri.

"Why did you do a commercial for John Engler?" Blanchard asked Alaassri, a Yemen native who has been a waiter at the famous downtown Detroit eatery since coming to America 14 years ago.

Alaassri sheepishly replied: "I did not know it was to be for John Engler."

An Engler campaign film crew approached Alaassri on Aug. 17 and asked him to appear in a TV ad. Alaassri believed the 30-second spot would promote the restaurant.

"I wanted publicity for business, I was not doing it for money," said Alaassri, who was not paid for the commercial.

As the commercial ended, Alaassri appeared holding a Vernor's and a hot dog on a plate. He spoke his only line,

"Two-twenty-five," his words laced with a Middle Eastern accent.

Alaassri is not eligible to vote, but he helped Engler in ways few others could. The spot he did was a humorous attack on Blanchard's property tax relief plan, which Engler claimed yielded only a nickel a week for each state resident. The savings for a full year would be enough to buy a hot dog and a soda, according to the spot.

That ad and others featuring the nickel-a-week slogan became a rallying cry for the Engler campaign. The nickel symbol was the highlight of a blockbuster, two-week period in October when Engler's effort to win the governor's office was revived.

Blanchard's media consultants said they had an ad prepared to rebut the nickel spot but opted not to use it because market testing told them the nickel commercials weren't working.

But the nickel ads were the most effective campaign commercial aired during the 10 months in which the two bitter political rivals waged a series of attacks and counter-attacks in a high-profile TV war.

The ad battle was launched in February, when Engler spots of uneven quality blamed the governor for everything from high unemployment to worsening pollution. The first commercials were produced on a shoestring budget by Dan Pero. They were designed to boost the challenger's name recognition and kick a little dirt on the governor at low cost, less than $75,000.

They were criticized as amateurish by everyone from media ad watchers to Engler allies.

Pero conceded that the early spots, and an accompanying campaign song entitled "Just Think What the Right Man Could Do", had a homespun feel.

"The criticism ticked me off a little bit, but I also knew we were still reaching our goals," Pero said. "We were within 14 points" by early September.

Pero eventually surrendered the ad production duties to Michael Murphy, a rotund, 28-year-old whiz kid from Washington who had done some impressive work for George Bush's 1988 presidential campaign. Pero said after the election that he regretted not having hired Murphy earlier.

Detroit Tigers first baseman Cecil Fielder started belting mammoth homeruns in the spring. But noticeably absent were any bleacher-reaching shots from the Blanchard campaign.

On May 14, the governor finally fired his first volley in the ad wars. It immediately backfired and became the first in a series of high-profile blunders from the Blanchard team.

The ad was called racially insensitive, racist and later, by Blanchard aides, "that (bleeping) ad."

The ad depicted a guard shouting first at a white convict and later at a black one in the state's military-style boot camp for young felons at Freesoil in northwest Michigan. Black inmates were pictured scrubbing floors while a white drill sergeant stood watch. The ad debuted in predominantly white outstate areas.

The 30-second spot set off an avalanche of controversy, first from Republicans, then from black lawmakers and the NAACP. The governor was playing to white outstate voters, the critics said, attempting to show that he was tough on black criminals from Detroit.

Black legislators met May 16 behind closed doors in Rep. Nelson Saunders' Lansing office to review a tape of the ad. Rep. Morris Hood of Detroit could be heard from the lobby screaming his objections to his fellow lawmakers.

"He (Blanchard) figures we have nowhere else to go," Hood bellowed.

Better than eight of every 10 Detroit voters who showed up

at the polls in the last two elections for governor had voted for Blanchard. The governor was taking the black voters for granted, Hood was saying. Maybe this time they just won't show up, he warned.

Blanchard already was on shaky ground with blacks, who saw him as neglectful of urban and black issues. The boot-camp spot was another example of his insensitivity to black citizens, black lawmakers said. Even many white lawmakers were shocked, demanding that the governor pull the spot from TV.

Blanchard and his campaign aides disputed the racism charges, saying the commercial was a realistic portrayal of the racial makeup of the boot camps. They insisted they had planned all along to run the spot in Detroit. The ad eventually had a brief run in the Metro Detroit area, but that ad time was not purchased until after the controversy surfaced.

"Leadership types may have had one kind of reaction to the boot camp ad, but the average voter, whether in Detroit or Macomb County, said 'Right on, it's time someone did something,'" said Bachula. "Every poll we did, every focus group we did said the boot camp ad was a very strong positive for us."

The boot camp ad was the brainchild of Robert Squier, the renowned, Washington-based political ad guru for Democrats and Blanchard's TV consultant in 1986.

When it comes to negative political advertising, Squier is known as the Prince of Darkness. The Blanchard campaign went nasty early and stayed that way for six months. That surprised many political veterans, who thought that the two-term incumbent would stress his accomplishments, make personal appeals to the voters on TV and remain gubernatorial.

Bachula said he and other campaign advisers saw little choice but to blast away at Engler. Ad money spent trying to plant new opinions about Blanchard, a well-known eight-year incumbent, would yield marginal payoff, the campaign staff reasoned. But Engler was a blank canvass.

"We decided to spend a significant amount of our time and resources trying to paint the Engler picture and never letting him paint himself," Bachula said.

Bachula had "seen the future" during a Thanksgiving 1989 trip to Boston to visit his wife's family. The Boston Globe carried a series of stories about voter disgust with sitting politicians. Bachula clipped the series, copied it and handed it out to the A-team.

Campaign advisers realized they were going against conventional wisdom that said incumbents in Michigan need only to remain above the fray and force the challenger to come to them. But the raging anti-incumbent mood made this a different kind of race, Bachula said.

"We thought being gubernatorial distances you from the average person who's ready to strike out somewhat indiscriminately," he said. "So there was a risk to a strict Rose Garden strategy.

"What we ended up doing was a combination in which we tried to keep the governor as gubernatorial as possible, but the campaign, the party, the surrogates took on Engler in hand-to-hand combat."

As a result, Blanchard did little of the personal campaigning that marked his earlier elections. At the same time, Bachula, Treasurer Bob Bowman, Budget Director Shelby Solomon and other Blanchard lieutenants launched vicious attacks on Engler. Bowman referred to Engler as "eye to eye with worms in the gutter."

While all this was going on, Michigan TV viewers watched Squier pound Engler relentlessly in 10-second and 30-second commercials. To counter the throw-the-rascals-out undercurrents, the ads tried to cast Engler as a typical lying politician whose 20 years in the Legislature made him more incumbent than the incumbent governor.

45

"We were most worried about the 'time for a change' theme," said Bill Knapp, the ad man at Squier's firm who did the Blanchard campaign. I thought their nickel ads were clever, but not really effective. If they had hammered "time for a change' for eight months, they could have won by 10 points."

The Squier barrage should have been no surprise to anyone in Michigan who paid attention to the 1989 campaign to pass Proposal A, the ballot proposition to raise the state sales tax by a half-cent to fund schools.

Blanchard supported Proposal A, and Bachula, his campaign manager, was given the task of getting it passed. Bachula hired Squier.

Few thought it possible to find a way to use a negative ad in support of a school finance measure. Squier proved them wrong. His ads ridiculed the Legislature for its handling of public school funds. He used language in the spots that was so misleading a lawsuit was filed challenging their accuracy.

"We tried to tell the people running the Proposal A campaign that the negative ads weren't working, that we had to get the message across how schools would be better for your child if it passed. Instead, we picked on the state Legislature," said Allan Short, chief lobbyist for the Democratic-dominated Michigan Education Association.

Proposal A was soundly defeated by voters. But the Blanchard team was still commited to Squier, and to negative advertising.

In the 1990 campaign, scripts were written for a variety of spots boasting about the administration's pet programs. The campaign had found a high school dropout and single mother in Grand Haven who was saved by a Youth Corps job. They had lined up a young couple with a new baby whose college tuition had been prepaid through the governor's Michigan Education Trust (MET) program. A-team members such as Bowman pushed hard for a MET ad. In the

46

state Labor Department, Blanchard allies lobbied for ads bragging about the Youth Corps.

But the commercials never aired, nor did Michigan voters see Blanchard talking to them in TV spots. Those kinds of spots were considered right up to Election Day, Bachula said.

"There's a general sense among voters that 'a lot of government spending goes somewhere other than to my family,' " Bachula said. "The danger of focusing on a few of the governor's programs is that it might actually reinforce that feeling. We didn't have enough money to run 20 such ads to cover the waterfront. So we didn't do any."

Said Knapp, of Squier's firm: "We would have liked to talk more about what Jim Blanchard had done and wanted to do. But we also had to talk about our opponent, and, with the spending restrictions, you can't do both."

Focus groups, paid panels of ordinary citizens asked to view and comment on the effectiveness of ads and campaign messages, told Blanchard aides that the governor did not come off well on television.

"Nuclear," was the word one aide used to describe Blanchard's effect on focus group viewers. The panels also responded cynically to positive messages.

"I sat through the focus groups and saw how people reacted to the positives," said Katie Wolf, press secretary for the Blanchard campaign. "We have a very cynical public out there. And every time we put a positive spot up, we lost points in our polls."

On Aug. 2, Iraq invaded Kuwait and stunned the world. Five days later President Bush sent the first wave of U.S. troops to the oil-rich Middle East.

The Blanchard team was wary about what the international crisis might mean to Michigan's auto-driven economy and to voters' attitudes about their candidate.

But in mid-August, the campaign had other pressing concerns. They were hearing a growing chorus of complaints from their friends about the negative ads and how they were turning people off. Bachula, Blanchard, pollster Tubby Harrison and state Democratic Party Chairman F. Thomas Lewand met at the governor's mansion on Mackinac Island to discuss whether to continue the negative onslaught. They decided to stay the course.

"It turned out be a meeting where we reaffirmed our strategy," Bachula said. "We also decided if there was some positive messaging, it should be in the populist mode. So we looked at big oil, keeping gas prices down. We also looked at auto insurance companies and rolling back rates. Taking on the establishment."

And keeping the top guns trained on Engler.

Squier, and Rothstein & Associates of Washington, D.C., the ad firm hired by the Democratic Party, were well-equipped to do that job. A Squier ad for James Florio in New Jersey's 1989 race for governor cast opponent Jim Courter as Pinocchio, his nose growing with every lie.

Here's a sample of Squier's Michigan work: "John Engler. . . a dangerous record on crime." "John Engler works only a day and a half a week." "John Engler voted to raise his own pay." "John Engler. . . just another politician." "John Engler. A change for the worse."

How low were the Democratic ad whizzes willing to go? Jeff McAlvey, Engler's studious-looking, bespectacled legislative aide, found out.

McAlvey was heading for lunch on Aug. 10 when he answered a phone call from a group that claimed to be a freelance film crew from Nebraska working for the Smithsonian. They said they were preparing a piece on state capitol buildings that were being refurbished, and could they please take some footage of the recently restored Senate chambers?

McAlvey assigned an aide to take them on a tour and went

to lunch. His phone rang again at 2 p.m. It was Jerry Lawler, the aide who escorted the film crew.

"I think you've got a problem," said Lawler. "All they wanted to do was shoot John Engler's desk. They polished the desk and pointed the nameplate toward the camera."

Lawler got all names and addresses, but none of them had business cards. A woman in the crew gave her name and an address in Nebraska. She turned out to be Kelly McMahon, daughter-in-law of Bob Squier and an employee of Rothstein & Associates.

"I realized the type of people we were up against," said McAlvey. "There was no line that they were unwilling to step over."

The hard-line ad strategy was solidified in the 1988 presidential race between George Bush and Michael Dukakis. Dukakis was widely criticized for failing to respond to negative ads aired by Bush depicting a polluted Boston Harbor and blaming Dukakis for furloughing Willie Horton, a convicted murderer who committed rape after his early release.

"We were attempting to raise questions about his (Engler's) credibility," said Bachula. "So that by October, if he makes arguments against us, people don't believe him."

Some of the Blanchard missiles scored direct hits. Engler aides conceded that the ad charging the Senate majority leader had a poor attendance record in the Senate did heavy damage. Another spot quoting Mt. Pleasant natives saying Engler is a bad neighbor also battered the challenger.

Bachula said the Blanchard game plan was based on the assumption that Engler eventually would have to go negative to win.

Engler did go negative. But he did so without getting any mud on his own shoes.

It rained on the Coast Guard parade in Grand Haven on the morning of Aug. 4. Engler and his aides were soaked.

By afternoon, the rain had stopped. The candidate and his newly hired ad man, Michael Murphy, met on the deck of the Windward, a cabin cruiser moored in Grand Haven and owned by the parents of campaign political director LeAnne Redick. Dan Pero and Redick joined them for sandwiches, crackers, beer and political brainstorming.

The group decided the ad campaign should focus on property taxes and education with "time for a change" as the overriding theme. They also talked about attacking the "imperial governor" and exploiting the nickel.

"The nickel ad wasn't designed that day, but we talked about it as a symbol and decided it was a winner," said Murphy.

Murphy, a native of Grosse Pointe Park, cut his political teeth doing media for the National Conservative Political Action Committee, which represents the right wing of the GOP. He also did time with Roger Ailes, the architect of the Bush attack ads aimed at Dukakis.

For the Engler ads, Murphy took the candidate out of his suit coat, put him in blue button-down oxfords, loosened his tie and rolled up his sleeves. He also had Engler's eyebrows trimmed and advised the candidate to shed a few pounds.

Murphy said he didn't want to tamper with Engler's looks too much because he "has that regular guy appearance. And that was a contrast for us against Blanchard's slickness."

It was decided to shoot most of the spots from Aug. 16–19. Along with the Lafayette Coney Island commercial, they set up a commercial blasting Blanchard for flying to the governor's residence on Mackinac Island in tax-supported jet planes and helicopters. Murphy crews filmed a Clara ("Where's the Beef?") Peller-type woman screeching "Two-fifty!" in reference to Blanchard's paltry property tax relief plan.

The nickel ads were completed in Leland Kenower's back-yard in New Jersey. Kenower is a friend of Murphy's who has a special high-speed camera that was used to show a cascade of nickels falling slow-motion to the bottom of the TV screen.

Then another decision was made that had the potential to be disastrous: The ads would all be saved for a big push in October.

CHAPTER 6

Hell Month

Engler aides called September "the month from hell."

It started off well enough for the challenger. He had cut Blanchard's lead to about a dozen points, according to the polls.

The Republican convention on Sept. 7–8 was uneventful, exactly how Engler had scripted it. By the time the convention opened, the entire Republican slate had been hand-picked by Engler and none was challenged by delegates.

That same weekend in Flint, Lt. Gov. Martha Griffiths sabotaged the Democratic convention. News stories focused on her unceasing criticisms of Blanchard and her refusal to attend a Sunday tribute planned in her honor.

"I don't think anybody really figured out what Martha wanted," said Katie Wolf, press secretary for the Blanchard campaign.

Griffiths earlier had consented to the tribute and the program was all arranged. But she backed out, and made scathing remarks about Democratic leaders.

"I hate to hear a bunch of hypocrites up talking," she said, when asked why she didn't want the tribute to go on as planned.

She also chastised the governor on Connie Chung's national network interview show on Sept. 10.

"I didn't know that Martha was going to do what she did, or Paula was going to do a book. It was an unusual year," Blanchard said.

But soon after, the momentum swung back to Blanchard and away from Engler. Two days after the convention, Engler delivered one his worst speeches of the campaign before the Economic Club in Grand Rapids, the hub of his GOP base. The speech was too long, lacked focus and the audience became restless. Many left early.

"He was exhausted that day. We had several late events the day before and a couple before the noon luncheon in Grand Rapids," said David Bertram, Engler's aide and driver. "He just didn't have it."

Early in the month, Bertram was slapped with his only traffic ticket in 120,000 miles of campaign driving, a speeding citation on I-696 near Farmington Hills. It proved a bad omen.

During September, the state Democratic Party shelled out $1 million for a barrage of negative television ads attacking Engler. Before it was over, the party would spend $3 million against Engler, said Party Chairman Tom Lewand.

The Republicans, having decided earlier to save their ammunition for October, did little to respond. Blanchard's lead began expanding in the internal polls.

Engler's campaign strategy was questioned by some staffers and morale ebbed. Even loyal Engler backers were telling reporters they thought the race was over.

"By the end of September, I seriously questioned whether John could pull this thing out just because it seemed the only strategy here was to lay on the ropes and let the other guy punch himself out," said Robert LaBrant, a lawyer and political expert for the Republican-controlled State Chamber of Commerce.

"In September, I thought if you let these people land all these blows on you and not punch back, the charges are going to be believed."

Polling done by Marketing Resource Group, a GOP consulting firm in Lansing, found Engler's popularity among voters dropping in legislative districts around the state.

"Everything seemed to collapse," said the firm's President, Tom Shields. "The attendance ad, the Mt. Pleasant ad hurt. Everything just took a dive. It was horrible."

Engler said "it took patience" not to counter punch in September.

"During that period I told people who asked questions: 'Understand this, you can lose September and win October and win the election. But if you win in September and lose October, there is no way to win the election.' "

The plan to lay low in September wasn't some master stroke of strategic brilliance, however. The state GOP figured it didn't have deep enough pockets to go dollar for dollar with the Democrats, whose war chest was swelled by union contributions.

"We knew we couldn't match them blow for blow," said David Doyle, executive director of the state GOP. "We decided, 'let's hold our fire.' "

Blanchard spent much of the month blasting big oil companies for raising prices at the gas pump and promoting legislation to bar the petroleum giants from owning and operating gas stations in Michigan. He also made several trips to schools promoting his computers-in-the-classroom program and appeared in Pontiac to witness the National Guard tearing down a reputed crack house.

Both got the governor a lot of favorable, and free, media attention.

A Detroit News poll published in early October confirmed that the month had taken its toll on the Engler campaign. Blanchard had widened his lead to 26 points and was ahead everywhere in the state. Other polls reported similar margins.

"It was tough waking up," said Dennis Schornack, Engler's chief policy aide. "John called us into his office and said the polls are wrong and here's why. He said we were down, but not that far. He said you're tired. You've been working very hard. But you've got to suck it in and work even harder and believe we're going to win. If you do, we're going to win."

On the Blanchard side, the governor and his aides were buoyed by what they saw as their strongest month of the campaign.

"We had a very good September," said Curt Wiley, a director of the Democratic Party campaign. "We had strong media, strong programs. But in October, everything started to go crazy."

CHAPTER 7

No Sex, but Lots of Lies and Videotape

"On the issue of protecting the environment, you're a Johnny come lately, aren't you Senator?" asked John Kost, doing his best Jim Blanchard imitation.

"No. I'm not," replied John Engler in the mock debate at GOP headquarters in Lansing. "And when Johnny comes marching home again, we'll have the solution to this."

The staffers groaned and rolled their eyes.

"You're not really going to say that on statewide television, are you?" one Engler aide asked.

In an Okemos TV production studio dressed up as a debate stage, Blanchard was trying to keep up with Treasurer Bob Bowman, who was playing the role of John Engler.

Bowman and the Blanchard debate team were detailing a string of tax-hike votes cast by Engler during his two decades in the Legislature and suggesting one-line zingers Blanchard could dish up.

"Slow down Bob," Blanchard said. "Let me get this. . . how did you say that?"

So went the candidates' practice sessions for the first debate on Oct. 6 in Traverse City. In the three televised debates in the 1990 race for governor, the candidates strived for snappy sound bites delivered with a comedian's timing. The truth of what was said was less important than the delivery.

The October debates shed little light on the combatants' records or on their visions for the state. Instead, viewers saw hour-long mirror images of nasty Engler and Blanchard campaign ads. The debates lacked zip and spontaneity, and also the knockout punches each candidate had hoped for. In short, they were dull.

By design and Blanchard's insistence, few people watched the debates. Two of the three were on public TV only, and the first and third contests were shown on Saturday nights when viewers were tuned into other activities. Blanchard knew that he had the most to lose and Engler the most to gain.

The debates had little influence on the campaign. The far livelier exchanges came between the candidates and the media.

The first wave of campaign TV ads made it clear that Engler and Blanchard intended to spend most of their time and money shellacking each other in 30 second commercials.

The ads from both camps were filled with half-truths and bald-faced lies. Absent from the ads was much talk about issues: improving education, cleaning up the environment, reducing crime and drugs. These discussions generally were limited to newspaper editorial board meetings, or to a series of issue papers from Engler, and Blanchard's 72-page "Strategy for Michigan's Future."

But both candidates urged the media to focus on those meager issue scraps and leave the television advertising, and their records in office, alone.

Instead, the state's largest daily newspapers decided to play truth squad on the TV ads.

The Detroit News took apart the ads in stories that

John Engler and Michelle de Munbrun savor a few private moments before being interviewed by the press in San Antonio. Audrey Shehyn Photo

John Engler and Michelle de Monbrun answer questions from the press at the Maison del Rio hotel in San Antonio. Audrey Shehyn Photo

Longtime friend
Colleen Pero hugs
Michelle after her
wedding to John
Engler in San Anto-
nio. Audrey Shehyn
Photo

John playfully kisses
Michelle, his new
bride, in their East
Lansing condo.
Audrey Shehyn
Photo

Michelle picks pine needles off John's sweater after he crawled under the Christmas tree to correct it's crooked slant. Audrey Shehyn Photo

Paula "chose to believe" that her husband was telling the truth, when he told her he was not having an affair with Janet Fox even though they married after Blanchard's divorce. David Coates Photo

Barbara Listing said the only way the Right to Life PAC would endorse Engler was if he would put it in writing, a promise to sign a bill outlawing all abortions, except to save a mother's life, should such legislation ever come before him. 1985 James Varon File Photo

John Engler's Oldsmobile was the vehicle — and the symbol — of his journey to the governorship of Michigan. In the final days of that journey, he spoke at the Leland High School, where a student asked if he had driven his Olds. After the assembly, he led a procession to show off the vehicle. George Weeks, Detroit News Photo

Agnes Engler appeared in a commercial responding to John saying his own mother wouldn't vote for him if "half of what Jim Blanchard says about me was true." Agnes and Matt Engler in their Mt. Pleasant home. Audrey Shehyn Photo

1948 family picture of a 3-month-old John Engler.

John Engler and Connie Binsfeld celebrate their victory at 5:00 a.m. after an election night in which the lead changed several times. Audrey Shehyn Photo

John Engler shares
an emotional
moment with his
father, Matt, on
election night.
Audrey Shehyn
Photo

Governor James
Blanchard held a
press conference the
day after elections
and said he might
want a recount.
David Coates Photo

Jubilation begins to permeate the Engler staff and close supporters as the final results come in. Audrey Shehyn Photo

Election night John Engler with running mate Connie Binsfeld are obviously enjoying the moment. Audrey Shehyn Photo

On election night,
John Engler contem-
plates the signifi-
cance of his victory.
Audrey Shehyn
Photo

John Engler
announcing official
acceptance after his
stunning upset
against incumbent
Governor Jim Blan-
chard. Audrey She-
hyn Photo

appeared throughout the campaign. One article asked, "How can you tell when John Engler and Jim Blanchard are fibbing? When the camera starts rolling."

The Detroit Free Press began a series under the standing headline "Ad Watch," a column that described the ads, offered analysis of the content and detailed any distortions of fact.

"Engler casts governor as likable idiot," one Ad Watch said of an Engler commercial. A Blanchard anti-crime ad was "dangerous to the truth," the newspaper said.

In the middle of the campaign, The News published a series of articles that revealed how the Blanchard administration had doled out $183 million in state contracts to contributors, former aides, party activists and Republicans who had helped the governor.

The stories pushed the governor and his lieutenants into a rage.

They took the unprecedented step of buying an ad in suburban Detroit newspapers to rebut the stories and trash "The Republican Detroit News" under the headline, "Anatomy of a Smear." The ad cost $15,645, money taken from the governor's officeholder account.

"If you prefer your news laden with facts, find it in some other newspaper," the ad said. "You might enjoy the change. They contain fewer errors. And certainly less arrogance."

On the Sunday before the election, Blanchard took out another newspaper ad to list the names of hundreds of people who could be expected to support a Republican, but instead were backing Blanchard. The full-page ad on page 11A of The News blasted the paper for endorsing Engler.

"Unlike this newspaper, they've put performance over partisanship," the ad charged.

Although they ignored the age-old warning against picking a fight with someone who buys ink by the barrel, both newspaper ads reflected a basic strategy position adopted early in the campaign by the Blanchard team: No charge would go unanswered.

Blanchard insiders said some campaign staffers were nervous about running the ads for fear of drawing more attention to the stories.

"We concluded, 'What do we have to lose?' " said state Budget Director Shelby Solomon.

Engler had his own problems with the press. Stories revealed that an inactive oil well owned by his brother, Jim, was spewing pollutants into the soil in mid-Michigan. Another detailed Engler's connections to a conservative think tank that used contributions from Republicans to chastise Blanchard programs.

By mid-October, Engler's whining about the lack of issue coverage had become incessant.

"If they (the Detroit daily newspapers) had done more front page stories on taxes and schools it would have been a lot more helpful to the public in terms of knowing about the candidates," said Engler.

But when asked late in the campaign why he didn't buy issue-oriented print advertising, Engler mumbled, "Our studies indicate that isn't the best use of campaign dollars." Engler appeared to be adhering to his 1970 philosophy that issues mattered less than image.

Robert H. Giles, editor and publisher of The News, said the candidates' attacks on the press indicate the newspaper touched the right nerves with its coverage strategy.

"Our campaign coverage was influenced by two factors: what the candidates did and the newspaper's own enterprise," Giles said. "Blanchard and Engler shaped their campaigns and committed large amounts of money to attacks on each other, in debates, on the stump and in television ads.

Our task was to sort out fact from fiction, to inform voters about the lies and half-truths that were at the heart of the campaign strategies. Engler released his school and tax programs before sparse crowds in out-of-the-way places, a tactic that seemed designed to divert attention from them. The News covered the proposals and ran columns and editorials commenting on them, but the candidates never pushed their ideas for solving Michigan's problems to the top of the campaign agenda.

"As a result, there was little else the newspaper could do to sustain discussion of these issues. The News aggressively pursued stories from our Lansing Bureau that raised serious questions about millions of dollars in state contracts by the Blanchard administration. This enterprise was a significant part of our coverage because it informed readers about the performance of the governor. The fact that the Blanchard people over-reacted to our stories suggests that we were on to something."

Engler was also given to overreaction and outrage particularly by the campaign polls conducted for The News by Gannett Corporate Research. The final poll on the Sunday before Election Day showed him 14 points behind Blanchard.

The next night, Engler appeared on WJR-Radio's all-night talk show to complain that the poll did not reflect the endorsement of him made by The News' editorial board. He also griped that the wording of the poll favored the incumbent.

"On polling, the newspapers just flat out don't know what the hell they are doing," Engler said. "They do a disservice to the public by trying to create news. By spending their funds to hire a poll, they've bought themselves their own story and then play it as if it's reality instead of covering the issues in the campaign."

The final News poll did overestimate Detroit voter turnout, which most likely showed Blanchard to have a larger lead then he had at the time.

But after the election, Blanchard said it was he who was hurt by the poll, claiming it kept his supporters at home.

CHAPTER 8

A Love Story

The blonde lawyer with a Texas drawl seemed out of place at the Michigan Republican Convention in early September, when John Engler was welcomed by the 3,300 delegates and alternates as the party's candidate for governor.

She was literally waiting in the wings on the stage at Cobo Hall as Engler, tears welling in his eyes, thanked his party and introduced his parents, Matt and Agnes. Only a handful of Engler's closest friends knew that Michelle DeMunbrun, a 32-year-old Houston bankruptcy lawyer, had accepted Engler's proposal of marriage made the weekend before.

Engler first saw his future bride in July 1989 when DeMunbrun stopped by Engler's Lansing office while visiting her best friend, Colleen Pero. Pero and DeMunbrun had been colleagues at a Houston law firm and a lasting friendship developed. Engler and DeMunbrun spoke only briefly that day. He gave her a Detroit Tigers baseball cap.

"I tease him about that day and say he doesn't remember meeting me, but he says he does," DeMunbrun said.

The second time the couple met, again briefly, was in the parking lot of a Grand Rapids restaurant when Colleen Pero and DeMunbrun met Engler to exchange cars while he was on the campaign trail.

Engler and DeMunbrun next met in Miami Beach in mid-April. Dan and Colleen Pero had planned a rendezvous with DeMunbrun that weekend. Deciding their candidate was in serious need of a campaign break, they invited Engler to tag along.

Engler and DeMunbrun shared breakfast in a cafe on the beach, dined in an Argentinean restaurant and fell in love.

"We just hit it off really well," DeMunbrun said. "Even coming back to Texas I didn't know what it would turn out to be. But I knew it was special."

Win or lose, they set a wedding date for Dec. 8. Her impact on Engler was profound.

"I'll never forget the state convention when John cried as he introduced his parents," said Dick Posthumus, an Engler pal since college days. There was a warmth there. I had never seen that John in public. It started coming out, and he wasn't afraid to show it.

"I think it was all connected to his engagement to Michelle. His life was becoming whole again. Everything was coming together for him. He started feeling and showing it. That helped him in the campaign, too. It helped that the warmth came across."

DeMunbrun said she and Engler talked long-distance every night.

"He would tell me stories about what happened that day," DeMunbrun said. "He has such an inner drive that he kept himself going. I guess I'd like to think that I helped him keep going, too."

As Engler was falling in love, Jim Blanchard was paying the price for falling out of love.

Did Jim Blanchard cheat on Paula, his wife of 21 years? Was Blanchard a neglectful husband and father who cared only about politics?

Paula Blanchard strongly suggested the answers to both questions was "Yes" in a book timed to arrive at the peak of political interest. Paula Blanchard's, 'Til Politics Do Us Part, was excerpted in The Detroit News for five days in late July and early August. Blanchard had tried to talk his ex-wife into delaying publication until after the Nov. 6 election. Instead, it hit book stores on Aug. 6.

Although not nearly as tantalizing as originally billed, a couple of vignettes in the book were especially damaging. One painted Jamie (she used that nickname throughout the book and it was gleefully adopted by Blanchard's detractors) as a political junkie who had little time for his wife and son.

"If you think I got elected to Congress so I can babysit while you go to school, you're crazy," Paula quoted Blanchard as saying in 1975 when she proposed attending classes at American University. To do so, Blanchard would have had to take more responsibility for their son, Jay, who was in kindergarten.

The book also told the story of a Blanchard trip to the Grand Caymen Islands in March of 1987, one he asked Paula to skip. Paula later found out that Janet Fox, the governor's secretary and long-rumored love interest, was on the Caribbean island as well.

Alone at home, Paula phoned several friends and asked point-blank "if Jamie and Janet were having an affair?"

Each answer she received only heightened her suspicions.

"No one laughed and screamed 'Are you serious? Are you kidding? Whatever gave you that idea?' No one said, 'No.' "

Several nights later Blanchard flew back into Lansing. As

he began to unpack his bags, Paula confronted him. "Are you having an affair with Janet Fox?"

She recalled the governor responded instantly: "No I'm not. I'm very fond of her and we are close, but we are not having an affair."

Paula said she chose to believe that her husband was telling the truth, even though Blanchard married Fox after their divorce.

Time magazine, The New York Times and USA TODAY all ran stories, which were unflattering to the governor, about the book. John Engler kept quiet. His own first marriage had failed, and ex-wife Colleen Engler was also working on a book, titled A Matter of Trust.

There were similar suggestions that Engler had been unfaithful and obsessed by politics. One report published in November after the election quoted Colleen's mother, Katie House, as saying that the book alludes to marital infidelity.

"I would have tarred and feathered John Engler two years ago, but there's no sense in carrying around a lot of anger," House said.

But unlike Paula Blanchard, Colleen Engler didn't publish her memoirs.

CHAPTER 9

A Secret Promise

Abortion was expected to dominate Michigan's 1990 race for governor. Few topics in 20th Century politics have so polarized the electorate or stirred such raw emotions.

On no issue were the positions of Gov. Jim Blanchard and challenger John Engler more clearly defined, or so diametrically opposed.

The issue had tremendous momentum. In 1989, Democrat James Florio rode his pro-choice stand into the New Jersey governor's office, as did Democrat Doug Wilder in Virginia. The U.S. Supreme Court in July of 1989 gave states much broader power to limit abortions, and court watchers were predicting that the justices eventually would overturn Roe vs. Wade, the landmark 1973 case that legalized abortion everywhere in the United States.

In Michigan, anti-abortion groups were beginning a drive to enact a law that involves parents in their daughters' abortion decisions. Blanchard, long a supporter of legal abortions, became a spokesman for the National Abortion Rights

Action League. He was a keynote speaker at the group's October 1989 conference in Washington. During his years as governor, he vetoed numerous attempts by the Legislature to end Medicaid-funded abortions.

Engler was just as strongly committed to the pro-life stand. Although he was never the point man on abortion legislation, the Senate he led passed dozens of abortion limitation measures that were vetoed by Blanchard. The Engler-Blanchard race promised a showdown on the issue.

But unlike other states where gubernatorial candidates made abortion a major issue, Engler and Blanchard generally avoided it in public for fear of galvanizing the opposition.

Engler had seen how the involvement of pro-choice groups in Virginia and New Jersey had tipped elections in favor of Democrats. Blanchard was wary that the issue would be defined in Michigan as parental consent. Voters were much less sympathetic to his stand on parental consent than on the much larger issue of whether abortions should continue to be available in the state.

Only in front of obviously friendly audiences, such as the party conventions, did the candidates attempt to rally the troops around their abortion stands. Abortion was not mentioned in a single TV campaign ad.

Polls also showed that the issue was not moving the electorate. In a September Detroit News poll, only seven percent of respondents said abortion was the most important matter facing the state, well behind crime and drugs, education, jobs and taxes.

"I think abortion is an issue that a lot of average citizens find to be so difficult and so painful that they don't want to have it shoved in their faces," Bachula said.

"It's not something we'll take the offensive on, but we won't hide from it either," said John Truscott, spokesman for the Engler campaign.

Although the issue was not on the cutting edge of the race

68

for governor, the organizations that worked both sides of it were.

John Engler needed an army. Right to Life of Michigan wanted a commitment. Both got their wish.

The 23 members of Right to Life's political action committee filed into the organization's Lansing conference room on Aug. 28. Engler was on the agenda seeking the organization's endorsement. With it would come a volunteer network numbering 35,000 who would plant yard signs and make phone calls for favored candidates.

Right to Life had demonstrated its clout in 1988, when its legions convinced voters to end tax-funded abortions in Michigan, and again in 1990, when they collected enough signatures to force the parental consent law.

"I'm pro-life," Engler told the political action committee board. "My position has been consistent for 20 years."

Some PAC members were annoyed, others downright angry when Engler told them he would support a "tightly written" law that outlawed most abortions, but kept them legal for victims of rape and incest.

Members protested that their position was that all of the unborn should be protected, regardless of how they were conceived.

The meeting, sometimes emotional, dragged on for an hour. In the end, the board gave its blessing to Engler. It was not unanimous, and came only after Right to Life President Barbara Listing reminded her top field soldiers of a letter Engler had given her before the meeting.

In the letter, Engler promised to sign a bill outlawing all abortions, except to save a mother's life, should such legislation ever come before him. That type of law goes much further than the rape and incest position Engler was espousing on the campaign trail. The promise was never publicized, but Listing said it will not be forgotten.

"We would not have endorsed him without that commitment, in writing," Listing said.

While Right to Life and its 125 local organizations canvassed the entire state, pro-choice groups focused on Oakland County, considered to be a bastion of pro-choice Republican women.

The Michigan Abortion Rights Action League formed in the summer of 1989, jumped into its first statewide political campaign only a few months later.

The national headquarters funneled about $100,000 to the group to be used primarily to buy time on Oakland County cable TV and to make phone calls to Republican women in the county on behalf of Blanchard.

But the group's get-out-the-vote effort paled in comparison to the massive Right to Life campaign. Even the abortion rights group's leaders conceded that.

"Frankly, our opposition has been at this for 17 years. We've been at it less than 17 months. This was our first foray, our first election. We learned a lot," said Carol King, Executive Director of the pro-choice group.

Blanchard staffers questioned the commitment of pro-choicers.

"Where were my very good friends who were involved in the choice movement?" asked Julie Dade, the governor's Detroit office director. "There was some national activity. But there weren't the volunteers, not the people who were so concerned because Engler was anti-choice. I wondered where they were."

The pro-choice group was "out of its league," said another Blanchard staffer. Right to Life, by comparison, was a battle-tested, disciplined, single-issue outfit that had been organizing its membership and fighting since Roe vs. Wade in 1973.

King said media and internal polls curbed the pro-choice effort in Michigan. Had the polls shown the race to be close, the national organization would have pumped more money into the state, she said.

King said "it sure would have helped" if Blanchard had centered on the abortion issue on the campaign trail or in TV ads.

"We never said it was the silver bullet, but it turned the tide in Virginia and New Jersey," she said.

A disillusioned Paul Hillegonds bumped into Jane Muldoon at the Right to Life of Michigan dinner Oct. 23 in Holland. He had lost hope for an Engler win. Muldoon helped change his mind.

"John can win," Muldoon told Hillegonds. "Here's some reasons why"—1.66 million reasons.

Through its nearly two decades of fighting to end abortions, Right to Life had identified and banked in its computers a list of 415,000 Michigan households that support its cause.

Muldoon, head of the organization's PAC, told Hillegonds that Right to Life planned to send three mailings to each of its targeted households and to follow up with phone calls to get their backers to the polls.

Right to Life paid for and helped distribute 52,000 Engler yard signs. They also handed out literature for Engler and other candidates at dinners attended by 400 to 1,300 supporters in Jackson, Novi, Traverse City, Holland, Grosse Pointe and Holland.

Then, a week before the Nov. 6 election, roughly 35,000 Right to Life volunteers went to work at phone banks in their homes and in branch offices around the state.

"We had an army of people out there. We were in every county," Muldoon said.

Altogether, Right to Life said it spent about $250,000 on Engler. Bachula doubted the figure, saying it had to be much more.

At 4 p.m. on Election Day, exit polls showed Engler and Blanchard deadlocked. Engler telephoned Listing at Right to Life headquarters in Grand Rapids.

"Keep up your calls. We're in a dead heat," Engler told her.

CHAPTER 10

Nickels, Jetcopters & Mom

If any one day symbolizes the shifting of the campaign's momentum from Jim Blanchard to John Engler, it has to be Thursday, Oct. 25.

John Engler's plan, his message and luck had meshed.

Engler campaigned from daylight to midnight in southwest Michigan, reminding voters that in 12 days they would choose between change or more Jim Blanchard.

Following his plan to the letter, Engler, with driver Dave Bertram at the wheel of the Oldsmobile, made 21 separate campaign stops in southwest Michigan. He pumped thousands of hands.

In Battle Creek, he greeted union workers at the General Foods plant gate. He dropped in at Central and Lakeview high schools and at a branch of Michigan National Bank. He toured the Ralston Purina Co. In restaurants along a local strip, he interrupted diners to ask for votes.

He went on to Kalamazoo, where he toured International

Paper Co. and local hospitals and made his pitch to editors of the Kalamazoo Gazette.

"It was the best day of the campaign," Bertram said. "We hit a lot of coffee shops and restaurants, and the reception that day was tremendous. John was handing out nickels and people were responding well. It really pumped us up."

The day typified the last three weeks of Engler's campaign.

"He seemed to be everywhere," said Dennis Cawthorne, a Lansing lobbyist, Engler friend and former state House Republican leader. "In the closing weeks, my hometown newspaper in Manistee carried stories and pictures of Engler three times. He had gone there three times.

"That was more than Blanchard had in eight years."

Blanchard, meantime, was also in Kalamazoo facing the newspaper editorial board and in Detroit for a luncheon speech to the Economic Club. The governor, of course, had flown to both stops on a state plane.

To reinforce his message, Engler and the state GOP unleashed a new batch of campaign ads on statewide television.

On that Thursday, when viewers switched on the Today Show, the evening news or Wheel of Fortune, they saw Naji Alaassri at Lafayette Coney Island reminding them of the paltry Blanchard tax plan. When they turned on Cosby, they saw a model airplane zig-zagging across a crude map of Michigan, a cartoon Jim Blanchard at the controls.

The spots were taking their toll on Blanchard. Don Koivisto, a Democrat who won a Senate seat in the Upper Peninsula, said the plane ad scored in the western Upper Peninsula, where car travel is a fact of life.

"I tend to think some of Engler's catchy commercials with the airplane and nickel hurt Blanchard, the airplane one in

Governor-elect Engler enjoys his waning hours as a senator in the state senate chambers with Sen. Harry Gast. Audrey Shehyn Photo

Engler chats with fellow members of the senate as the term draws to a close. Audrey Shehyn Photo

Engler called his last press conference as a state senator. The next press conference he calls will be as the governor of Michigan. Audrey Shehyn Photo

John Engler, the face of determination. Steve Haines Photo

Before the inaugural ceremony, John and Michelle Engler attend church with father, Matt Engler. David Coates Photo

John Engler receives a congratulatory hug from his wife, Michelle, after being sworn in as Governor. David Coates Photo

John Engler is sworn in on the Capitol steps in Lansing. Audrey Shehyn Photo

"The torch is passed . . ." Jim Blanchard offers his best wishes to the new Governor. David Coates Photo

During the inauguration of John Engler, former Governor Jim Blanchard and his wife, Janet, take a moment to ponder their future. David Coates Photo

John and Michelle Engler, dancing at the inaugural ball. Detroit Institute of Arts. Audrey Shehyn Photo

John Engler hugging Ethyl Thompson, known as grandma Ethyl, 82, of Mt. Pleasant. Audrey Shehyn Photo

John and Michelle traveling between Traverse City and Mt. Pleasant during the inauguration week. Greg Domagalski Photo

Governor and Mrs. Engler with John's mom Agnes greet supporters at a reception in Mt. Pleasant. Audrey Shehyn Photo

Governor and Mrs. Engler take delivery on their "new" 1991 Oldsmobile at the G.M. factory in Lake Orion. David Coates Photo

particular," said Koivisto, whose district is as far from Detroit as Detroit is from Washington D.C. "A lot of people said, 'Hey I drive. I can't afford to take a plane. Everybody drives.' "

And the Michigan Republican Party opened its vault, finally, and spent $1.1 million on TV and radio ads for Engler.

The two most visible spots funded by the GOP were slapstick TV ads produced by Marketing Resource Group. The 30-second spots masked their negative message with a humorous delivery, a stark contrast to the acerbic tone of the Blanchard ads.

In the first, a film crew went to MSU's Forest Acres West golf course, where they dressed three of their own staffers in black and white prison stripes and another as a guard. As the convicts putted leisurely, the narrator accused Blanchard of running country club prisons.

"It's time to get Michigan back on the right course and get the criminals off the golf course." The truth-stretching ad played off a putt-putt course being built with inmate money at a Muskegon prison.

In the second ad, a black-and-white video tape showed scenes that conjured up images of the bungling Keystone Kops. As old roadsters drove over bumps in the road, the narrator told viewers it had been a "rough ride" with "Blanchard at the wheel in Michigan." The ad closed with a car hanging over a cliff. "Blanchard's been in the driver's seat. Michigan is out of control. Time to turn the keys over to someone else."

Meantime, the much more serious Blanchard and Democratic Patry ads accused Engler of favoring numerous tax hikes and supporting price-gouging oil companies. "Maybe it's best when John Engler doesn't show up at all" for work, said one ad. "John Engler. Big oil. Perfect together." Another commercial used a scrapbook to sum up all the attacks launched on Engler in the campaign.

Six days before the election, Engler came out with a 30-second spot aimed at debunking the negative attacks. Speaking directly into the camera, he said his own mother wouldn't vote for him if "half of what Jim Blanchard says about me was true." The commercial cut to his mother, who said: "Oh, I was voting for you all along, John." Corny, no doubt, but it got the desired response from test audiences.

Agnes Engler told a visitor to her rural Mt. Pleasant home: "That ad seemed silly when we were doing it, but I guess it turned out OK."

The strategic goal of the Engler campaign and state party was to show the ads so frequently that regular TV viewers saw each spot six to 10 times. This campaign year, that cost about $150,000 per ad.

Oct. 25 brought another sign of Engler's improving political fortunes. Ironically, it was at the expense of President George Bush, who won the White House in 1988 with Engler's help.

Newspaper headlines told of a compromise between the Bush administration and the Democratic-controlled Congress on slashing the federal budget deficit by $490 billion. It included $137 billion in tax increases.

Bush's signature on the final bill made him a liar and mocked his famous campaign creed: "Read my lips. No new taxes." Public opinion polls showed Bush's popularity plummeting.

That should have stung Engler, because of his close ties to Bush. But the federal tax hike added fuel to the anti-incumbent sentiment that was rocking governors across the nation.

It was a powerful and fortuitous development that broke Engler's way. His message, "I'll cut your taxes 20 percent" and "time for a change", meshed nicely with the mood of the day.

"He was the one out there saying 'government is wrong,' " said Shields. "He was the one saying 'I'm going to cut your taxes.' He was lucky enough to be in the right place at the right time."

Gary Bachula said the ugly mood of the electorate undermined the governor's campaign. Throughout the year, internal polls for Blanchard had found an alarming dichotomy: He was well ahead of Engler, but about half of Michigan voters thought the governor didn't deserve a third term.

"There's a national unrest and it was far more powerful than anything we did or anything they did," Bachula said. "People seemed to hold the governor to a very high standard and seemed to feel that he didn't measure up. They seemed to blame him for everything from job losses to high taxes to stealing the lottery money to paying too much attention to Detroit. But pervading it all was this incredible disgust with all politicians."

During the last five days before the election, Engler made more than 40 campaign appearances. His get-out-the-vote machine kicked into action. The 35,000 Right to Life of Michigan volunteers and thousands more working at Engler and state GOP phone banks in every county called more than 1.7 million voters in the final week.

Clear evidence of the impact of Engler's message and his surging campaign came on Friday before Election Day. He was speaking to students, parents and teachers in the gymnasium of Leland High School north of Traverse City. A girl kept raising her hand during his speech. Finally, she interrupted and asked: "Did you drive your Oldsmobile?"

"Sure did," Engler answered. "It's in the parking lot."

The crowd roared.

Detroit Mayor Coleman Young opened his Manoogian Mansion for a Blanchard reception on Oct. 26. Most of Young's appointees were there.

While mingling with the city officials, Blanchard said repeatedly: "Don't let the polls fool you. Don't let the polls put you to sleep."

Young told the crowd how important it was to get the Blanchard team elected. The governor delivered a short speech.

"The speech was nothing to get you all pumped up to go out and work for him," said Mildred Stallings, Democratic chair of the 1st Congressional District.

Young had turned over his political machine to the governor. But many questioned the mayor's enthusiasm and commitment.

When fully engaged, the Young machine has the power to help elect anointed candidates. In the past, it had sent sound trucks into the neighborhoods encouraging residents to vote, and provided shuttle service to the polls. Not this year for Blanchard.

It was no secret that the governor and Young had not been the closest of friends. Blanchard's programs to benefit middle-class suburbanites largely left Detroit behind. He had slashed human services, hurting the city's poor. He had been slow to back issues important to the city, such as reinstatement of Detroit's 5-percent utility tax.

On a number of occasions, the mayor had publicly questioned the governor's political courage.

"I have made some derogatory statements about the size of his testicles from time to time," Young said in the fall of 1989.

Before the governor's race got underway, the staffs of Young and Blanchard had met at a Brighton restaurant to improve relations. The meeting didn't help much.

Besides the Manoogian reception, Blanchard and Young met at least two other times during the campaign. They huddled on Aug. 28 at a private dinner at the Omni Hotel with Sen. Carl Levin and UAW International Ford Vice-President Ernie Lofton. And they met with Levin, Sen. Donald Riegle and Attorney General Frank Kelley at the Jaffe-Snider law firm on March 3, following the Democrats' Jefferson-Jackson dinner in Detroit.

By all accounts, the meetings were cordial and Young promised to do what he was asked. But he wasn't asked to do much.

"What we sought from Coleman Young was organizational support and we got it," said Bachula. "Coleman is a polarizing figure and he knows that, the governor knows that. Coleman Young did what we agreed was appropriate for this campaign."

Young made a radio ad for Levin and for the Democratic party, but Bachula said the mayor was never asked to do such a spot for Blanchard.

The mayor made a brief appearance at the Democratic convention in September and offered this lukewarm endorsement of Blanchard: "I'm a Democrat and I'm supporting the ticket. I don't think there's anybody here who's given enough attention to the problems of minorities and cities."

Also at the convention, State Rep. Morris Hood, D-Detroit, suggested Blanchard had alienated his Detroit base.

"I think the entire Democratic Party is guilty of forgetting its roots, and if that includes Mr. Blanchard, so be it. Many of the working people I know have talked about sitting this election out," Hood said.

Late in the campaign, the governor visited several black churches without the mayor. Blanchard's stops at the churches were not listed on his public travel schedule, which almost guaranteed there would be no media coverage for suburban and outstate voters to see.

The governor skipped a Young reception at the Manoogian following Nelson Mandela's visit to Detroit in June. He did not attend the Barrister's Ball in February, a major black social event, although Engler was there. He also missed a key Oct. 20 rally at a Detroit union hall that was attended by 700, including Young.

"The night before someone got a call saying Blanchard couldn't make it," said Stallings. "We planned the rally around the date that they said he was available."

Blanchard attended other rallies in Detroit, but he did little personal campaigning in a city that felt far removed from the governor, said Julie Dade, Blanchard's Detroit office coordinator.

"It was my suggestion that we go into neighborhoods in Detroit and that we talk to average citizens. . . which is what we did (once)," Dade said. "My hope was that we would attempt to do that in various ways throughout the campaign, which would have given people an opportunity to see the governor in a way they had not in the last four years. But we didn't."

Said Stallings: "The people are used to seeing door-to-door stuff. When they don't see it, they say, 'I must not be important enough.' You have to motivate people to go to the polls. We didn't do that."

Those who did go door-to-door on Blanchard's behalf said they met the dissatisfaction in person.

"I'm 35 years old, I've got three kids and I'm unemployed," said one Detroit resident called upon by a Democratic Party precinct worker. "You really think it matters to me whether Jim Blanchard or John Engler is the governor?"

Sen. Carl Levin was more than a half-hour late to the joint rally at the Macomb County Community College gym on Nov. 1, the Thursday before Election Day, leaving the governor nothing to do but stand around and wait.

Blanchard looked anything but gubernatorial.

A bout with the flu had forced him to cancel an appearance at a morning Democratic rally in Kalamazoo. At the evening rally in Macomb, he rasped through a speech chock full of populist themes.

Levin was tied up at another appearance. The already small crowd in the college gym was thinning fast.

"If it wasn't for the high school band, there wouldn't be anyone here," said Leo Lalonde, a Corrections Department official and an active Macomb Democrat.

Blanchard stood on the stage, shifting uneasily. A heckler shouted at the governor. Something about property taxes.

Strong winds, a cold driving rain and mixed reviews greeted Blanchard on Sunday morning, two days before voters would make their choice.

A front-page headline in The Detroit News blared: "Blanchard well ahead, 54% to 40%."

If you believed the poll, conducted Wednesday to Friday of the previous week, then you had to believe the race was all but won.

Alex Gage, a veteran GOP pollster and consultant from Southfield, didn't believe the poll.

"The public is very angry and upset, and they are going to punish somebody," Gage said.

An internal Blanchard poll, conducted Friday and Saturday, proved Gage a prophet. The results, also relayed to Blanchard on Sunday, showed his lead had shrunk to 5 points.

Later that day, Blanchard attended a rally in his hometown, Pleasant Ridge. The Oakland County bedroom community had been the launching pad for each of his three gubernatorial campaigns. Still dogged by the flu, Blanchard was met by a sparse crowd comprised mainly of staff, news reporters and party regulars at the city's community center.

"I knew we were in trouble when I looked around and I

knew everybody in the room," said Ann Beser, director of the Democratic Party's efforts on Blanchard's behalf.

It was the day before the election and Gary Bachula was a nervous wreck. He'd had little sleep since Blanchard pollster Tubby Harrison informed him on Sunday that the race had closed dramatically. Nobody was sure why it was happening or if the trend would continue.

It was too late to shoot new TV ads or to make radical adjustments in strategy. The only thing they could do was shore up their get-out-the-vote effort and hope the hemorrhaging would stop.

Bachula called party Chairman Tom Lewand about beefing up phone banks and mobilizing door-to-door precinct workers, especially in Detroit.

The governor was urged to do as many radio and TV interviews as possible, imploring his backers to go to the polls.

In an effort to pump a new sense of urgency into the campaign, volunteers were told the race was tightening. Passing thoughts of telling the media about the new numbers were quickly dismissed for fear of energizing Engler's supporters.

At midnight Monday, Bachula started to relax, knowing that the campaign was doing all it could. The phone rang. It was Tubby Harrison.

"Gary, are you sitting down? It's 47–47, a dead heat," Harrison said.

Bachula's heart sank.

On Election Day, John Engler awakened to the smell of a country breakfast in his parents' Mt. Pleasant home. In a couple hours, he would head out to vote at Union Township Hall, then drop by Stanley's Famous Restaurant to kibitz and pick up the coffee tab for a table of locals.

Voters throughout Michigan were on their way to the polls

82

to choose a new governor. Engler had relayed his message, stuck to his plan and triggered organizations in all 83 counties to get his supporters to the polls.

Engler glanced out the window at the steel-gray sky. He heard on the radio that up to 16 inches of wet snow had blanketed Republican-rich northern Michigan. From Kalkaska to Alpena, power lines were down and roads to the polls were impassable.

Later, a chance meeting with a custodian in a hallway at a Farmington Hills High School polling place buoyed his spirits. GOP Chairman Spencer Abraham, who was with him, overheard a school janitor answer flatly, "No," when a co-worker asked if she wanted to meet Engler.

"Sick of politicians?" Abraham interrupted.

"No. Just sick of incumbents," she said. "I did vote for a couple, Frank Kelley and Dick Austin."

"Did you vote for Engler?" said Abraham.

"Yeah, but that doesn't mean I want to meet him."

Engler and Abraham headed to Lansing to wait out the night with supporters at the Radisson Hotel. Abraham seated himself at a long table, took out his tally sheet and began making notations in blue and red ink.

After voting at the Pleasant Ridge Community Center, Blanchard had breakfast at the Rialto Restaurant in downtown Ferndale.

Armed with new poll numbers, he visited phone workers at his campaign office in Ferndale.

"We've got to get them out," Blanchard told his volunteers. "This is going to be a close one."

More bad news came in a 3 p.m. phone call from Greg Hicks, who was running the Democratic Party's get-out-the-vote effort in Detroit.

"Turnout is low, very low," Hicks reported. Turnout in the city would never climb above 34 percent.

Aides scrambled to get Blanchard on TV and radio. He went live with TV-7's Bill Bonds at 5 p.m. An hour later, he did several live interviews on radio stations oriented to black listeners. The Democratic Party had purchased the radio time and even fed a set of favorable questions to disc jockeys.

On a day most pundits thought would find Blanchard relaxing, the governor instead hustled for votes.

At dusk, a weary Blanchard headed to the International Center at Greektown to join his staff and supporters.

When the polls closed at 8 p.m., all three Detroit TV stations pronounced the race too close to call. Blanchard settled in for a long night.

CHAPTER 11

It's Over

Jim Blanchard tried to appear upbeat as the vote-counting ordeal dragged on, but aides could see he was worried.

The governor half-joked about this night being like 1982, when he went to bed not knowing whether he or Richard Headlee would be governor. It was nothing like 1986, he thought, when he was ready to declare victory as soon as the polls closed at 8 p.m.

Peter Graham, a Blanchard Aide, busily punched returns into a personal computer in a private office in Greektown's International Center. At 3:55 a.m., numbers taken over the phone by Tom Scott hit the governor like a telegram bearing news of death. With only 8 percent of the state's precincts not counted, Engler was still ahead. The precincts still out were in Republican strongholds.

Blanchard studied the figures for a moment and his face went gray. He turned, said nothing, and walked away.

"I'll never forget that moment," said Curt Wiley, a Democratic Party official who witnessed the unseating of a governor.

Blanchard met Bachula in the hallway and put his arm around his close friend and adviser.

"Gary, we did everything we could," Blanchard consoled.

Although the outcome appeared certain, the tally was so close that Blanchard and his team would not publicly concede the race to his long-time enemy. Talk turned to the possibility of a recount, should the final margin be no more than a few thousand votes.

Blanchard aides told stragglers at the party downstairs that the race was still too close to call and that everyone should go home to get some sleep. They said there was still a chance the governor could pull it out.

But they didn't believe what they were saying.

"It's over. We're out," said Bill Castanier, a Labor Department spokesman and Blanchard activist. He and Labor Director Betty Howe briefly embraced and walked quickly out of the hall.

Others at the party offered epitaphs for the campaign.

John Patterson, a Blanchard volunteer from Highland Park, said of the low turnout in Detroit: "People went to sleep on the job. They just assumed Blanchard would win and they underestimated the challenger."

Blanchard was driven to the Radisson Hotel Pontchartrain and went to bed about 4:30 a.m.

John Engler was sleeping at 5:30 a.m. in his suite at the Lansing Radisson. Downstairs, Spencer Abraham's impromptu victory statement spread through the candidate's election night headquarters like an August brush fire. The crowd of Engler backers roared.

Abraham saw the same result in his numbers that Blanchard had seen in Greektown. Precincts from around the state that had not yet been counted would go to Engler, and he would win by at least 7,000 votes, Abraham figured.

"Everyone was shouting and screaming and crying and saying 'Did we add it up right?' " recalled Dennis Schornack. "Connie Binsfeld stayed the whole night, and she was crying."

Colleen Pero hurried off to the elevator to break the news to the candidate.

She knocked softly, several times. No response. She knocked harder.

"Yes?" came a voice from inside.

"John, we won! We won! We won! We won!"

Engler showered and dressed quickly, and at 5:50 a.m. went downstairs to declare victory.

"Tonight's a win for the taxpayers of Michigan," Engler said. "Jim Blanchard's mandate is going to be to find something else to do."

Engler and a small band of his closest aides headed up to his suite to reflect on the stunning upset. There were still traces of doubt.

The phone rang at 7:30 a.m. Colleen Pero answered. It was Michael Murphy.

"So how's it going?" Murphy asked.

"Well, we won," she answered. "Spence says we're going to win by 7,000 votes."

At that moment, an election update crawled across the bottom of the TV screen. The Associated Press had Engler up by just 600 votes.

The Engler aides exchanged looks of uncertainty. Colleen Pero looked at her husband. "Dan, we won, right?"

Dan Pero looked at Jeff McAlvey, and said: "Yeah, we won. I think we won. Jeff, did we win?"

"Yeah," McAlvey said. "We said we won, so I guess we won."

At 10:30 a.m., 13 hours after his last public appearance, Blanchard staged a news conference on the top floor of the Pontchartrain. About 30 aides waited for the governor in the large, window-lined room overlooking the city that had abandoned Blanchard the day before.

Aides gave their boss a standing ovation that lasted more than a minute. Eyes swelled with tears.

Blanchard appeared drawn, his usually well-tanned face was pale.

He quietly apologized to the media for keeping them up all night. But he still refused to concede, saying he wanted to review the numbers to determine if there was a reason to request a recount.

"If this razor thin margin holds up for John Engler, I will be the first to congratulate him," Blanchard said, and rushed out of the news conference to a nearby elevator, refusing to field questions from the press.

Campaign manager Gary Bachula stayed behind to answer a few questions.

"We may be paying a bit of a price for all the tax increase shenanigans in Washington," Bachula said.

He also acknowledged the effectiveness of Engler's commercials.

In the elevator down to the hotel lobby, deputy press secretary Lisa Grayson, who had checked her emotions throughout the news conference, broke down and wept.

Engler did not appear on the Today Show. The interview was cancelled because the election outcome was in doubt at the 7 a.m. air time.

At 2:45 p.m., Engler received a call in his Capitol office. It was Blanchard.

"Congratulations, John," a tired Blanchard said over his

car phone. "I'm committed to making this a smooth transition, and I'll do anything I can to help."

Both men called 3 p.m. news conferences.

"The people have spoken," a visibly shaken Blanchard told reporters at the Capitol Building. He ducked out again without answering questions.

"I sort of feel sorry for the guy," said one reporter after the beaten governor's brief concession speech.

Upstairs, several hundred people packed a legislative committee room, waiting to greet Michigan's 46th governor. Preliminary returns had Engler winning by 19,000 votes.

The triumphant and giddy Engler, wearing a dark suit, with running mate Connie Binsfeld at his side, strolled to the podium, stopping often to shake hands. The deafening applause lasted several minutes.

"How sweet it is," he shouted. "In January, there will be a new team in charge in Michigan."

In a private moment back in his office, Engler pulled out the tally sheet that Abraham used to call the race.

On it, he scrawled: "Spence, a dream come true! Many, many thanks!"

EPILOGUE

Three weeks to the day after the election, in a wood-paneled room a short walk from the Capitol, John Engler officially became governor-elect.

With a large, color photograph of James Blanchard peering down over their shoulders, the four-member Board of State Canvassers unanimously certified the results from Election Day that showed Engler the winner. He had carried 61 of 83 counties.

For the first time in 38 years, Michigan would be governed by a man who failed to get a majority vote. Engler netted 49.8 percent of the 2.56 million votes cast while Blanchard got 49.1 percent.

William Roundtree, the 40-year-old nominee of the World Workers Party, got 28,091 votes, depriving anyone of a majority.

Among those who captured some of the 1,800 other write-in votes cast for governor were comedian Pat Paulson, consumer advocate Ralph Nadar, Mickey Mouse, Pork E. Pig and Martha Griffiths.

By the time the board of canvassers meeting ended, the race for governor had tightened. Engler had won by 19,000 votes, according to the unofficial tally released the day after the election. But after paperwork errors were corrected, Engler's victory stood at just 17,595 votes. About 2.6 votes per precinct.

The final tally: Engler/Binsfeld received 1,276,134 votes; Blanchard/Maynard got 1,258,539 votes.

The Blanchard campaign spent $3.6 million, buttressed by $3 million from the state Democratic Party. That's $5.24 per vote. The Engler campaign shelled out $3.6 million, with the state GOP kicking in $1.1 million. That's $3.68 per vote.

The final numbers showed the Democratic governor had done well in Detroit, where he got 86 percent of the vote. Blanchard's problem was that only one-third of eligible Detroiters bothered to show. In his 1982 victory, Blanchard received 115,000 more votes in Detroit than he got in 1990.

Atty. Gen. Frank Kelley, Secretary of State Richard Austin and U.S. Sen. Carl Levin, the other Democrats at the top of the statewide ticket, won by lopsided margins. So only Blanchard felt the personal embarrassment of defeat. He got more than 300,000 fewer votes than he did in his two earlier wins and far fewer votes than other statewide Democratic candidates drew this time.

Bachula, Blanchard's campaign chief, had this to say about why Blanchard lost:

"What the Republicans say now about knowing all along their strategy would put them over the top is baloney. Two things beat us: The 'time for a change' feeling among voters and a good, organized effort at the end by Right to Life."

Asked why the Blanchard campaign stuck with a negative campaign, he said:

"We tested the basic comeback message and people said, 'Fine, you did a good job for us eight years ago but what have you done for us lately?'

"Focus groups laughed when we told them we created 650,000 new jobs. 'Can't be true, we haven't seen them,' they said. Because the economy was teetering that couldn't be true. As we searched for additional positive messages, we found areas of utmost concern to people, like education and taxes. They didn't want to hear new ideas or new proposals or agendas from an eight-year incumbent. Their only question is, 'Why didn't you do it?'

"My disappointment was that we hoped to take (Engler's campaign staff) off their course of action. I give them credit for sticking to their game plan and not responding to a lot of our ads. But we assumed we were in a win-win situation. If they responded we'd take them off course. If they didn't respond, then the negative information would stick. It ended up being a wise decision by them not to respond to us.

"We tried to tell people that he was no better than we were. We didn't think the nickel had any impact at all. But when we look back on it now, what they were saying was Blanchard hasn't done anything, he's promising very little, and anybody can do it better than that. Why don't you give us a shot.

"We saw no significant change in polls on the airplane and nickel ads until the very end. Maybe we needed to come up with some symbol of Engler being in session only 1 day a week, something equivalent to the nickel. Something we could hand out to reinforce it.

"In our heart of hearts we never thought we'd lose. Up to Thursday before the election I was very confident. Over the weekend I grew very frightened and nervous and anxiety ridden. It was too shocking an idea to move into my brain until election night."

State Elections Director Chris Thomas is troubled by the disappointing 45-percent turnout of registered voters on Election day. Turnout was down by more than 400,000 from the number of voters who could be counted on to cast ballots in the late 1970s and early 1980s.

"You can't help but wonder whether people feel more removed from government today and whether a growing number of them don't even know if government impacts their lives and if who is elected governor really makes a difference," said Thomas.

Blanchard pollster Tubby Harrison said post-election analysis shows that blacks, young people and liberals stayed home on Election Day. The last time those groups showed up at the polls in Michigan, he pointed out, was for Jesse Jackson in the 1988 presidential primary.

"You have to give them a reason to come out," he said.

In post-election analyses, the nation's media didn't know what to make of Engler's upset win in Michigan. The pre-election day focus had been on hot races in California, Texas, Florida and in North Carolina, where a black man was running for the U.S. Senate.

In a single paragraph of a lengthy article summing up the results on Election Day, Time magazine concluded of Michigan: "In some cases, women exerted more influence on the outcomes by their absence rather than their presence. Blanchard was tossed out by voters who were irritated by, among other things, his less-than-courtly dumping of Lt. Gov. Martha Griffiths, 78. His ex-wife also made a contribution to his defeat by selling her titillating memoirs to The Detroit News."

The New York Times missed the winner altogether. In a round-up of offbeat election results, under the headline "Best Soap Opera," the newspaper wrote that Blanchard was hurt by his ex-wife's book but noted that Engler's former wife, Colleen, decided to withhold publishing her book. "A kind gesture, but not a shrewd one: Mr. Engler lost, which could dampen the enthusiasm of the publishing world."

Engler never saw the piece. He was busy planning a new administration and family. On Dec. 8., before a small gathering of family and close friends in Texas, he and Michelle DeMunbrun wed. The night before, while shopping for ties in downtown San Antonio, Engler got a taste of what he can expect during the next four years.

"Aren't you John Engler?" asked an unfamiliar woman.

Gary Calder, a state police bodyguard for Blanchard who has taken command of Engler's security detail, had witnessed similar scenes with Blanchard countless times before.

"Anyplace you go in the world from now on, at least one person will recognize you," Calder told Engler.

Gov. Blanchard used his state-owned Lansing residence in early December to hold a farewell party for key staffers and the reporters who had chronicled his ups and downs during eight years in office.

Blanchard and his top aides often fought with the press during his years in office and during the campaign. Even after the final results had been tallied, the governor blamed his loss in part on the polls published in the last week by the Free Press and The News.

It was just one of many places he put the blame during his post-defeat depression. In the days following the election, he also blamed lackluster pro-choicers, the anti-tax advocates and others.

At the farewell party, the drinks were stiff and the mood more relaxed than many had expected.

"Stick around, I'm about to give my 'You won't have Jim

Blanchard to kick around anymore' speech," Blanchard joshed.

Lisa Grayson, anticipating the question of the evening, had penned on her name tag: "No, I haven't found a job yet."

Nancy Austin Schwartz, Blanchard's deputy chief of staff, summed up the year she will never forget. "I turned 40, had my first child and lost my job. The baby was great. The rest sucked."

After the election, Blanchard confessed that he had serious doubts about seeking a third term as late as February 1990.

"I got a very uneasy feeling about 1990. The UAW and the Michigan Education Association had boycotted my fund-raiser in May. The Legislature was tired of me. The press was tired of me, and (aides) said, 'Yeah, what's the alternative? Who is it the Democrats can run at this point?

"They were saying if you leave, you're annointing Engler, the guy who fought everything I have tried to do.

"I don't see how I could fault the people for not giving me a third term when I agonized myself."

Bachula headed for Disneyworld a few days after the election. He didn't bump into Dave Doyle, a key Engler strategist and soon to be Republican Party chairman, who had decided to gather up his family and do the same. But Bachula wasn't able to block the election from his mind.

One morning, while reading the Orlando Sentinel, he noticed that Patti Woodworth, a one-time Engler confidante who had taken a job as budget director in Florida, was heading back to Michigan to be Engler's budget chief.

"I can't get away from this stuff anywhere," Bachula said.

In the nation's capital, Mike Murphy finally found some time to hang the pictures and mementoes that had littered the

96

floor of his Georgetown office throughout the busy election season.

The 28-year-old ad man should become an even hotter property because of his key role in Engler's upset win in Michigan. On Election Day day, Murphy's political clients around the country went three wins, two losses and one that Murphy wants to put into the "no-decision" category. That was in Minnesota where GOP gubernatorial hopeful Jon Grunseth dropped out nine days before the election after being dogged by charges that he had skinny-dipped with teen-age girls a decade earlier.

"Some things you just can't anticipate," Murphy said.

Fifteen minutes away from Murphy's office are the offices of millionaire Democratic advertising guru Robert Squier. The loss of his Michigan client, Jim Blanchard, isn't likely to harm Squier's well-established firm. The Blanchard race was one of only two losses for Squier, against 11 victories.

Squier is credited with devising the ad strategy used by Democrat Ann Richards in her come-from-behind victory in the Texas race for governor. That drew national headlines. Ironically, during the campaign Richards was forced to withdraw one Squier-produced TV spot. It had altered headlines to make it appear that a newspaper, not Richards, was criticizing her opponent, millionaire businessman Clayton Williams.

Perhaps even more ironic, Republican Engler's new mother-in-law, Margaret DeMunbrun, boasted the day after the election that she had cast her ballot for Richards, a Democrat.

Spencer Abraham, decided after the election to step down after eight years as chairman of the Michigan Republican Party. During his tenure, he wiped out a $400,000 debt, devised a strategy to win control of the state Senate and helped Engler win the governor's race.

Abraham now will concentrate full time on his job as deputy chief of staff for Vice President Dan Quayle, a job he held at the same time he was at the helm of the Michigan GOP.

Blanchard's Cabinet of Bachula, Solomon and Bowman had announced no future plans.

Dan Pero began moving his people into the offices those three once occupied and reflected on what was perhaps the biggest political upset in Michigan history.

"I've never seen a more tenacious, aggressive campaigner than John Engler. He has incredible personal skills, and he can go from dawn to midnight without ever stopping," Pero said.

"We knew that they were very smart people, particularly the governor. We knew that Blanchard's team would react by not leaving any charge unanswered. There was not a personal bond that existed between Jim Blanchard and the people, like there was with Bill Milliken. Blanchard was shallow. He stood for nothing except public relations. He was a cheerleader. People would say, 'I'm voting for Blanchard because I don't know much about Engler' or 'I'm a Democrat.' Few could give us any strong reason, a real reason, for voting for him.

"We thought our ads were creative enough to cut through the clutter. We thought that if we could deliver a contrasting message, with a touch of humor to it, people would not look at our campaign as one that is muddy and negative. We felt that if we could get people chuckling and laughing at our opponent, it would play for us.

"Their whole ad strategy to beat on us was flawed from the start. If they had argued a reason to re-elect Jim Blanchard rather than trying to paint Engler as a change for the worse, they would have been much more successful.

"Their advertising at the end was one of the most pathetic endings I've ever seen during a campaign. When the race is tightening, you want your best stuff on. They had their weakest stuff on."

98

For Engler, there would be no honeymoon—not with Michelle, and not with the Lansing establishment.

In fact, eight weeks into his first term, he had a stranglehold on "the most hated man in the capital" title.

"Swift, savage, succinct," is how Sen. John Kelly, D-Detroit, described the administration's opening act. "It's been a radical departure from business as usual around here."

His proposals to chop spending rankled every human services and arts advocacy group in the state. Everywhere he went during the early months, Engler was met by hecklers and angry protesters toting picket signs.

While many slammed Engler's actions, no one called the new governor a slacker. Even his adversaries conceded he's shown a willingness to get out in front of his sweeping agenda to make the bold moves needed to achieve his goals.

"Actually, he's done too much," House Speaker Lewis Dodak, the governor's primary political adversary, said half-jokingly in February.

"I give him credit because he's eager to get in there and tackle a lot of tough tasks. But you have to look at the state from all angles, listen to all sides," said Senate Democratic Leader Art Miller.

The actions and priorities set during the first eight weeks reflect Engler's Reaganesque philosophy of government—smaller is better; reduced taxes will result in economic growth; welfare spending perpetuates poverty.

Engler and his minions went to work immediately devising a plan to balance the state's books and avoid a $1.1 billion deficit. The plan included $800 million in budget cuts that ended general assistance welfare payments to able-bodied adults; drastically slashed spending on the arts; and greatly reduced the size of government.

The governor also unveiled a 20 percent property tax cut proposal 15 days after taking office.

"He's certainly shifted the center of debate to a question of how government will be downsized rather than will it be downsized," said Hillegonds. "He also has shifted the debate from whether taxes should be raised during a time of tight budgets to how is the property tax going to be cut."

Craig Ruff, president of Lansing-based Public Sector Consultants, said Engler is pushing his agenda by forcing confrontation rather than the coalition-building approach that marked the Blanchard, Milliken and Romney administrations dating back 27 years.

"He's drawing the line, saying 'you're either with me or you're on the wrong side,' " said Ruff. "He understands that the old political center has evaporated and there are more conservatives than liberals in this state."

The governor said public outcry over the budget cuts was expected.

"A lot of the outcry is very carefully orchestrated by people who have a different view of government than the majority of taxpayers," Engler said, adding, "I'm comforted by the knowledge I only have to go through this once."

On Dec. 18, a relaxed Jim Blanchard studied the calender in his mind. Two weeks from that day, he would no longer be governor. As he told his office visitors, "I'm just a humble Oakland County voter who will try to help elect the next Democratic president."

The pictures, awards and other memorabilia on the office walls were numbered, so the movers could do a proper inventory. Blanchard said he thinks the man moving into the office will be up to the challenge of running the state.

"John Engler will do just fine," Blanchard told his guests. "Nobody ever turns out to be as bad as you think they will be."

CONTRIBUTORS

Roger Martin, 32, is Lansing Bureau Chief of The Detroit News. He is political and investigative reporter who also manages The News' nine-member state Capital bureau. A native of Ft. Thomas, Ky., Martin is a 1981 graduate of Michigan State University. He has received numerous awards for news and investigative reporting and feature writing.

Charlie Cain, 40, is the Chief Capital Correspondent in The Detroit News Lansing Bureau. Cain, a Detroit native, has reported for the newspaper since 1973, with a two-year break from 1980–82 to do television political reporting for the CBS affiliate in Detroit. A 1973 graduate of Michigan State University, Cain is also a prize-winning reporter.

Mark Hornbeck, 36, has been a staff writer in The Detroit News Lansing Bureau since 1989. Previously, he was a state capital correspondent for six years with an outstate newspaper chain. A 1976 graduate of Michigan State University and a Detroit native, Hornbeck has won awards for news and enterprise reporting as well as feature and education writing.

Yolanda W. Woodlee, 34, is a political reporter who covered the 1990 gubernatorial race and the 1988 presidential campaign for The Detroit News. She was born in Louisville, Ky. and graduated from

Rockhurst College in Kansas City, Mo. She worked for The Louis-ville Defender, The Fort Lauderdale News and The Miami Herald before joining The News in 1987.

George Weeks is The News' political columnist and author of four history books. During 14 years with UPI, he was Lansing bureau chief, and later for ex-Gov. Bill Milliken. Weeks was a Kennedy fellow at Harvard and is the author Stewards of the State, a book on Michigan governors.

Audrey Shehyn has been a staff photographer at the Detroit News since june 1990. She graduated from San Francisco State University in May 1990 with a degree in photojournalism. While there, she received the Greg Robinson Memorial Scholarship for outstanding photography. Shehyn was raised in the San Francisco Bay Area.

Nolan Finley, 36, is the Detroit News state editor, responsible for the coverage of Michigan politics, government and outstate com-munities. A native of Cumberland County, Ky., he graduated from Wayne State University and began work at The Detroit News in 1976 as a copy boy. He previously worked as a reporter in The News' suburban and City-County bureaus.

Mark Hass, 37, is an assistant managing editor at The Detroit News, responsible for city, suburban and state news as well as the newspaper's photography coverage. The Brooklyn native gradu-ated Magna Cum Laude in 1975 from the State University of New York at Buffalo. He also did graduate work in journalism and international affairs at the University of Maryland.